A PROSPEROUS FAMILY

A PROSPEROUS FAMILY
Strategies for Cultivating Lasting Prosperity and a Meaningful Legacy

NOTE: Definitions found in epigraphs and footnotes are from jpmorgan.com, irs.gov, or investopedia.com.

Securities and investment advisory services offered through LPL Financial member FINRA/SIPC. LPL Financial is separately owned and other entities and/or marketing names, products or services referenced here are independent of LPL Financial.

Expert
Press
www.ExpertPress.net

Editing by Ryan Huber
Copyediting by Hannah Skaggs
Proofreading by Geena Barret
Cover design and book design by Paperback Expert

A PROSPEROUS FAMILY

Strategies for Cultivating Lasting Prosperity
and a Meaningful Legacy

RJ Anderson, CPA
Foreword by Rob Anderson, CFP

To my beautiful wife, Michelle,
whose patience and unwavering support have allowed
me to serve my clients with the excellence I strive for
every day.

To my two children, Lincoln and Charlie,
whose love and encouragement have always been a
source of strength and inspiration.

To my parents, Rob and Julie,
who instilled in me many of the lessons that form the
foundation of this book.

To my incredible team
at Prosperity Investment Management, Inc., whose
dedication and support have made it possible for me
to devote the time and focus needed to bring this
book to life.

To my clients,
whose trust and commitment have not only inspired
this book but have also provided the purpose behind
my career.

And to my publishing team,
for their tireless effort and commitment in helping
transform this vision into reality.

With heartfelt gratitude,
RJ Anderson, CPA

CONTENTS

FOREWORD

As I write this foreword, I am filled with a deep sense of pride. For over forty years, my career as a Certified Financial Planner® has been a journey of dedication and growth. But one of the greatest joys of my life has been watching my son, a talented Certified Public Accountant, step into this world and bring his own skills and passion to the business I built.

From the beginning, I hoped that at least one of my children would follow in my footsteps and continue the work I started. There were times when it seemed uncertain, but today, I am fortunate to have two of my three children as financial advisors. My son has not only taken on the responsibility of leading the business but also made it stronger—enhancing our practice with his own expertise and vision.

What stands out most about my son is how he treats his clients like family. He always puts their needs first, ahead of his own financial gain. His passion for serving others is clear in the way provides advice and focuses on educating his clients. He understands that true financial success is built on knowledge and trust, and he works hard to ensure his clients feel informed and confident in their decisions.

His approach, with a focus on tax-aware and efficient management, brings significant benefits to our clients. The practice is thriving today, and I am proud of the way he has carried forward our legacy.

This book, written by my son, is a reflection of his journey. It's not a retelling of my story, but rather a new one, shaped by his experiences and insights. He has taken the lessons he learned from me, combined them with his own, and created a guide that will help anyone looking to build a prosperous and meaningful life.

What makes this book special is how it shares real-life experiences that are both relatable and insightful. These stories make the financial principles come alive, making the book not just a source of wisdom but also an enjoyable read. The lessons are practical, allowing readers to apply them to their own lives.

As you read this book, you will gain valuable insights into financial planning and wealth management, but also into living a life of purpose and integrity. My son's approach reflects a deep understanding that success isn't just about accumulating wealth, but about creating a lasting legacy.

I am honored to have played a part in his journey, and I believe the lessons he shares will resonate with you. It's my hope that you find inspiration and practical wisdom within these pages to help you build a future that is both prosperous and fulfilling.

Thank you for allowing us to be a part of your journey. I believe that the knowledge and insights my son offers here will help you take control of your financial destiny and create the legacy you envision.

With warm regards,

Rob Anderson, CFP

Founder, Prosperity Investment Management, Inc.

1
LONG–TERM STRATEGY

From Times Square to Wall Street

Long-term strategy: *a strategy that looks past the day-to-day fluctuations of the stock and bond markets and responds to fundamental changes in the financial markets or the economy.*

It's a four-mile walk from Times Square to Wall Street in New York City. Four miles exactly, if you take Broadway and the Avenue of the Americas (Sixth Avenue). To be more specific, this walk is from Dave and Buster's at Times Square to the New York Stock Exchange on Broad Street and Wall Street in Lower Manhattan. If you took this walk today, you'd pass landmark after landmark, including

5

the Flatiron Building and the Empire State Building. It might take you an hour and a half at a leisurely pace. For me, though, it took well over a decade.

Many years ago, I was ringing in the new year with the love of my life, Michelle, in Times Square. It was surreal. We've been married for over a decade now and have two kids, Lincoln and Charlie. Back then, we were just two explorers on a cross-country adventure, living in a small Toyota motor home, hopping from one Walmart parking lot to another. But we were steadfast in what we wanted. One of the things we wanted was to spend New Year's Eve together in New York City, watching the ball drop as we welcomed the new year. We just wanted to do it in the best way possible. I'll never forget weaving our way through those crowds, Michelle clinging to my backpack, police officers pulling us forward through the mass of people trying to gain last-minute entry to the Times Square party.

That's why we got the tickets months in advance to attend that party at Dave and Buster's on New Year's Eve. We did this so we wouldn't have to camp out in Times Square for days on end in the frigid December weather, only to stand in one of the cattle pens they had set up in the square. We wanted to do it in style, so we did our research, saved our money, and made our way across the country in eighteen feet of mobile "luxury." Sometimes, it turns out, the best way to be spontaneous and seize the moment is to plan for it in advance. How all this started is another story (or at least another chapter), but for now, just know that it was risky. It took some sacrifice and some planning and some saving, but it turned out to be a dream come true.

Another dream I've had, for a long time now, is to be part of the opening or closing ceremony on the floor of the New York Stock Exchange on Wall Street. In November 2023, that's exactly what we did. In many ways, it represented the culmination of all the years of study, hard work, and lessons I've learned along the way. Call it a long-term investment strategy. Not everyone gets to be a part of those ceremonies, with the ringing of the bell to open or close trading on that famous floor. I'm honored that I finally got to be a part of it. There were no guarantees that I'd ever get to make that four-mile walk. We took risks, made sacrifices, and learned a whole lot between Times Square and Wall Street, and I want to help others with the lessons I've been blessed enough to walk through over the course of this crazy life (so far).

This story doesn't really start in Times Square. It starts decades before that, on the other side of the country, in a small town called Chico, California. That's where I started as a kid, growing up, watching my dad, and learning the lessons that would help build the amazing life I have today. There, in and around Chico, I learned about taking risks, saving for the future, putting in the work, listening to people who had something to teach me, and putting first things first. The first person I learned those valuable lessons from was my dad, Rob Anderson, who had plenty to teach me.

Learning Lessons

- Take risks while you can. This is usually done when you're younger and have more time to course-correct if things go wrong.
- Mistakes made early in life are usually easily forgiven and have few long-term consequences. It's better to learn from small mistakes than big ones. It's even better to learn from other people's mistakes so you don't need to make them yourself.
- Make sacrifices to gain the things you really want.
- Sometimes the best way to be spontaneous is to plan for it in advance.

Burning Questions

- Is there something you really want, an adventure you want to take, or an experience you want to have that's worth risking, saving, even sacrificing for?

2
APPRECIATION

Watching Dad

Appreciation: *the increase in value of a financial asset.*

When I was growing up, my dad always ran family pictures in the newspaper every Christmas, but when I was born, he put a picture of me in the paper. The caption said, "Your future financial planner." And that was his baby announcement to the small town of Paradise, California. Everybody seemed to know him. And then again, when I was about two, there was an ice cream social in town, and I was on the front page of the *Paradise Post*, eating an ice cream cone. Again it said, "Your future financial planner" and talked about me being his son. Little did he know that it would eventually become true.

As a Certified Financial Planner® (CFP®), my dad started teaching me at a young age. When I was really little, he started a 529 account[1] for my college education. Maybe even more importantly, however, I remember when I first started getting my allowance. When my allowance was one dollar, I went to his bathroom sink, which was where he had his change. I can clearly recall standing at the bathroom counter and listening as he said, "Okay, your allowance is one dollar, and here's how it works: We're going to give you a dollar, but you're going to give ten cents to tithe. That's not all, though; the next ten cents goes to savings, and the next ten cents goes to taxes. So your dollar is seventy cents, and that's what you actually have to spend." (Unfortunately, due to rising taxes and progressive tax brackets, that seventy cents is even less today than it was then.)

---

[1] A 529 plan is a college savings plan that allows individuals to save for college on a tax-advantaged basis. Every state offers at least one 529 plan. Before buying a 529 plan, you should inquire about the particular plan and its fees and expenses. You should also consider that certain states offer tax benefits and fee savings to in-state residents. Whether a state tax deduction and/or application fee savings are available depends on your state of residence. For tax advice, consult your tax professional. Non-qualifying distribution earnings prior to 2024 are taxable and subject to a ten percent tax penalty. Beginning in 2024, unused 529 plan funds may be rolled into a Roth IRA assuming the following conditions are met: 1) must have owned the 529 plan for fifteen years, 2) can only convert funds that have been in the 529 plan for at least five years, 3) rollover amount cannot exceed $35,000 and 4) rollovers must be made to a beneficiary's Roth IRA.

That's how my dad showed me the value of a dollar. A dollar is seventy cents, and he gave me my introduction to this reality when I was a young boy. You don't live on the full amount you're making; you have to live on less. If I wanted a new game system or something like that, I would go out and buy that with my own money, and my dad would always say, "If you want it, you have to have the funds for it before you buy it. You can get it, but you're not going to get it and then pay me back. You earn the funds and then buy what you want to buy."

He taught me at this young age to prioritize saving for the future. He also taught me to make it automatic on the front end, before I had the funds and spent them. This is a similar idea to a 401(k).[2] If you make your contributions as part of payroll, before it goes into the bank, it tends to become automatic. You don't think about it. This is automating your future retirement. Once the money is in your bank account, it becomes painful to invest it. At that point, it's money that you have to "give up" in order to invest. Many people, when I tell them about this, have reasons they can't start investing in their future "right now." They tell me that they have other priorities they

---

2   401(k): a feature of a qualified profit-sharing plan that allows employees to contribute a portion of their wages to individual accounts, and those amounts are excluded from the employee's taxable income. Employers can contribute to employees' accounts. Distributions, including earnings, are includible in taxable income at retirement.

want to accomplish first, and then, once they start making more money, they'll begin investing.

This brings me to another important lesson: There will *always* be a reason to delay putting money into investments. It could be "I don't make enough yet" or "I want to buy a new car." Whatever that reason is, just know that once you meet that goal, it's highly likely you'll have another goal, and then another. This is why it's important to prioritize and start now—even starting with a small amount can make a huge difference when it's compounded over a career.

I took all of this in from a young age: I started mowing my neighbors' lawns to earn some extra funds. Another thing my dad did, as I started mowing lawns and earning money on my own, was talk to me about the future. He explained how when I grew older, I would want to buy my first car. So, to incentivize me for that, he did a couple of things.

First, he matched my contributions. As I recall, the minimum contribution was fifty dollars to my investment account. Therefore, if I put in a minimum of twenty-five dollars, he would match me dollar for dollar, which put a total of another fifty dollars into that account for me.

He also opened a dividend-bearing account[3] for me so that when we got our monthly statements, I could

---

3   Dividend: a portion of a company's profit paid to common and preferred shareholders. Dividends provide an incentive to own stock in stable companies even if they're not experiencing much growth.

see that I was getting paid on my money. By doing that, he taught me about compound interest,[4] the idea that putting my money away and investing it would make it grow. In that case, it doubled immediately, but there were limits on it. I couldn't put that money in and take it right back out to get the extra money that he was giving me. I had to keep it there for a minimum of three years to be "vested"[5] in the money that he was adding. This is also how he taught me the value of investing—that starting early and making steady contributions over time is how investments grow. You work for your money. Now have your money work for you. Eventually your money can earn more than you can.

I didn't just learn from what my dad told me, though; I also learned a lot just from watching him live his life. The value of hard work was one of the first and biggest lessons I took from watching him. So, at times, he would be working so hard that he essentially just came home to change clothes. He would come home late at night, fall asleep, and then be gone in the morning because he was so busy at some points. Of course, it wasn't always like that. He was definitely around during my childhood, but

4 Compound interest: the interest on savings calculated on both the initial principal and the accumulated interest from previous periods. "Interest on interest," or the power of compound interest, will make a sum grow faster than simple interest, which is calculated only on the principal amount. Compounding multiplies money at an accelerated rate. The greater the number of compounding periods, the greater the compound interest will be.
5 Vested: having rights to the full amount of some benefit, most commonly employee benefits such as stock options, profit sharing, or retirement funds.

at times he would be very busy. He just had to work hard, and he taught me that when you're the boss, you work harder than anybody else.

He also demonstrated that we don't finance purchases but wait until we can pay cash. We save and make that a focus. When it came to vehicles and things like that, he wasn't the guy who had a new car every year, or even every three years. He would drive that car until the maintenance got to be too expensive to justify keeping it. Although he had the means and the ability to buy a new car, he wasn't the flashy guy who always had a new one to show off.

Don't borrow money to buy a depreciating asset like a car or a vacation. It's okay to buy an appreciating asset like a home so that you can stop spending money on rent and build equity. By taking out a fixed-rate mortgage, you lock in your monthly mortgage payment and avoid future rent increases.

We also traveled all over the Western Hemisphere with Dad and his company because we went to lots of business events. When I was young, I went to Maui three times through his company. I started meeting other kids of financial advisors, and they were some of my first real babysitting jobs. I got certified as a babysitter at a young age. Once I was old enough to take on the responsibility, I babysat other financial advisors' kids at the conferences.

However, it wasn't all work and no play for my dad. When I was around eight years old, we had a houseboat that my family would practially live on in the summertime. Dad would sail the smaller boat back to the truck and tow it to his office for work. Then, in the evening, he'd put it back in the water and cruise out to the houseboat to relax and play with us. He would comment, "It was like being on vacation, but I went to work each day."

It was his work-life balance; people used to say that he worked harder and played harder than anybody else they knew. He would work long hours during the week, and then Friday evening we would take off and go do something. During colder months, he would come home, and we would load up in the truck and go to Lake Tahoe to ski on the weekends. We would come home late Sunday, and he would be back in the office Monday morning. Work hard, play hard. It was a lesson he learned from his parents and then passed on to me. I plan to continue the tradition and work hard to instill these values into my own children.

It was more than just his work-life balance. My dad lived an integrated life; it was all part of being a person of integrity, a person who was the same at work and at home, whether someone was watching or not. And we were watching. We weren't just watching Dad, either. We were watching my mom and dad *as a team*. We couldn't have lived the life we did without my mom taking care of all four of us, driving us where we needed to go, and saving money in all sorts of ways, including cooking most of our meals at home. My dad knew he had a team at home that made it all work together, and he had reasons he worked so hard. It seemed like some people worked really hard to make money they didn't even know what to do with. Dad, though, was a person who knew exactly why he wanted to make money.

It wasn't because he was a workaholic who didn't want to be around his family. He did it for us and to be with us. That's also why Mom worked so hard with us at home. And for us, for our team, it came down to experiences. These were something that he valued and that we valued as a family. My wife and I value them as well; we don't tend to spend much on material things, but we do spend it on experiences. This is because experiences and the memories they make are priceless when it comes down to it.

My dad was always there for the family. Like Mom, he was at my baseball games even though he was working hard. He came out to the lake, we enjoyed ourselves, and we were excited when he got off work to come be with us. There were times when we didn't see him as much because he was working so hard. During those times he would most often find a way to be really present and accessible. We appreciated all that Dad and Mom did to give us the childhood that we had together.

Learning Lessons

- Teach your kids about money early. Teach them how to save, teach them the power of compound interest, and teach them to live on less than they earn. Try your best not to take on debt.
- Allow your funds to grow; be patient. Good things take time.
- Learn from your parents and others, both the good and the bad. Then teach your children how to benefit from the good and avoid the bad.
- Work-life balance helps make life worth living. Your kids are watching and will learn from your integrity. There is no replacement for an integrated life.
- Some of the best teachers are not teachers.

Burning Questions

- What lessons did you learn from watching your parents or role models?
- What do you want your kids or younger people to learn from watching you?
- What good things in your life are worth being patient for?

3
GROWTH STOCK

The Almond Orchard

Growth stock: *a well-known, successful company that is experiencing rapid growth in earnings and revenue and usually pays little or no dividend.*

The almond orchard taught me the value of hard work. We moved out there when I was about twelve years old, and I spent several summers at home cutting, chopping, and stacking firewood while my family was on the lake. That was part of how I earned the money to buy my first vehicle.

Originally, my parents had bought an empty plot of land, and we were going to build a house there, but building that house became cost-prohibitive over time. It was just really expensive to build then, and the home would be worth significantly less than the cost to build it. While we were trying to figure out the plans for building that house, the almond orchard property became available. Dad had always dreamed of having his own barn. That was a big part of what sold him on the orchard—it had a great house and that big red barn. My parents decided to remodel the home and make some additions so that it would be their dream home.

At the same time we were preparing to move out there, while the construction was in process, my aunt and uncle's house burned down because of an attic fire, and afterward they were living in a hotel for a while. Because of all that, my mom decided to move us out to the ranch while our new home was being remodeled so that my aunt and uncle and their kids could live in our old home while theirs was being rebuilt. Dad agreed. For us, it was a fun new adventure.

My parents taught me that the way you treat people might be the most important thing. Investing in funds or accounts or real estate is one thing, but investing in people comes first. That's the kind of person my dad is: character and integrity are even more important to him than our financial health. We moved before the orchard house was ready, and we were living in a twenty-eight-foot travel trailer outside our new home, but we had access to the living room, a bathroom, and the kitchen

When we first started living out there, my dad began getting me involved in all the yard work, so I learned how to drive the tractors and mow the lawn. We got a riding lawnmower because there was a big lawn that went around the house, and then there was also the fruit orchard that we had to take care of ourselves. Dad would send me out there to pick fruit, mow the yard, and do all kinds of other jobs. Then, a year or two into living at the almond orchard, we had to "pull" that orchard and replant it.

The trees in an almond orchard last only so long. Their useful life of producing crops tends to be twenty to twenty-five years. At the end of that time, the trees don't produce as many nuts, and they start to die and fall over. At that point, when it becomes no longer feasible to keep going with the current orchard, the "pulling" process begins. After the trees are cut down, the workers bring in something that looks like a giant backhoe, and they grab the stump and pull it right out of the ground. They also have a big grinding machine, roughly ten feet across, that they drop the stumps into to turn them into chips. They then load the chips into semi-trucks and haul them away.

We had workers come in, and they chopped the trees off at the base and cut them up into firewood. They took all the small limbs and stacked them in a big burn pile, and stacked the usable firewood in rows. I had a little trailer that I hooked up to the tractor, and I towed it behind the workers. They cut the firewood, and I went behind them with the tractor and threw the firewood into the trailer. After that, I'd drive back to where we were stacking it and unload it, then split it and stack it. I spent most of the summer doing that when we weren't out on the lake as a family.

Eventually we replanted the orchard. There was some downtime after the pulling because we had to get the soil back into good condition. In the meantime, we grew some crops out there, like a kind of watermelon, but a type of watermelon you wouldn't normally eat. We would let it all grow and then die, and then the workers would till it all into the soil (that process took a year or two) for fertilization. After that, you replant. But, interestingly, the almond trees are actually spliced onto peach tree roots because the root systems are better, and so the stump is a different type from the rest of the tree. These are the kinds of things you learn working in an almond orchard.

Because of all this, throughout junior high and high school, I had the opportunity to work with some of the immigrant farm workers who were hired by the company that farmed our orchard. I got to see how hard they work, which was incredibly humbling. These were people doing backbreaking labor day in and day out, often for wages that most would consider far too low for the effort required. Yet, despite their circumstances, they carried themselves with dignity and resilience.

I remember eating lunch with one of them one day. He was an older man who had been doing this kind of work for years. During our break, he looked at me and said, "You need to go to college. You don't want to be out here doing what I'm doing for your entire life." It wasn't said bitterly or with resentment—he was encouraging me not to settle but to strive for more. That simple conversation stuck with me and shaped how I thought about hard work and opportunity.

What stood out to me was the sacrifices these workers made for their families. This man, like many of his coworkers, was working ten-hour days for wages that barely allowed him to get by. He lived in a small house crowded with other workers, yet nearly every dollar he earned was sent back to his family. He had chosen to endure the grueling labor and challenging conditions not for himself, but to provide a better future for his loved ones. That level of commitment and selflessness left a lasting impression on me.

It also became clear to me how much we, as a nation, rely on immigrant labor. They take on some of the hardest, least desirable jobs—jobs that many others simply aren't willing to do. These workers were out in the fields before I arrived, worked through lunch, and often stayed later than I did. Even as a young, energetic kid, I struggled to keep up with them. Their work ethic was unmatched.

One day, my dad and I were driving back from the orchard. We'd just finished pulling it and were busy cutting and stacking firewood. Along the way, we saw a man on the side of the road holding a sign that said, "Will work for food." My dad, always one to offer help, told the man, "We have a job for you. Come help us cut and stack firewood, and we'll pay you a fair wage." But instead of taking the opportunity, the man replied, "I'm not doing that. I just want the money."

That moment was eye-opening for me. It reinforced the lesson my dad had been teaching me for years: true charity isn't just handing someone money—it's providing them with an opportunity to improve their situation. Helping someone sustain a life of dependency isn't kindness; it's cruelty. My dad believed in giving people a hand up, not a handout, and I've carried that philosophy with me throughout my life.

Looking back, those experiences shaped my understanding of the value of hard work and the incredible contributions of immigrant workers. They taught me to appreciate the opportunities I've had and to work for a better future—not just for myself, but for others. It also deepened my belief that when we help people, we should aim to empower them, enabling them to create a more fulfilling and prosperous life.

I fully support helping people who want help, but I've seen that there are better ways to do it, and I learned that largely by working in the almond orchard. I also learned the value of hard work out there because I took what I earned and invested. Eventually that money paid for my first dirt bike, my first quad, and my first truck. We invested it in growth stocks, specifically a growth mutual fund[6] that helped my money grow faster than it would have otherwise.

That hard work was part of how Dad taught me that not all of my wants would just be given to me. I had to earn those things, and I had to save for them, even as early as twelve years old. I'll always remember buying my first quad with the funds I earned from mowing lawns, working in the almond orchard, and all the other opportunities I had to earn money through hard work and smart saving practices.

6   Mutual funds and exchange-traded funds (ETFs) are sold by prospectus. Please consider the investment objectives, risks, charges, and expenses carefully before investing in mutual funds. The prospectus, which contains this and other information about the investment company, can be obtained directly from the fund company or your financial professional. Be sure to read the prospectus carefully before deciding whether to invest.

Learning Lessons

- Investing in growth stocks is wise, but investing in people is the wisest thing you can do.
- Lead by example and learn from those beside you; no one is above sweat equity or better than the people working around them.
- Hard work can also teach you what you don't want to do forever; sometimes you want to learn to work smarter, not just harder. The harder I work, the luckier I get.
- Many times the difference between successful people and unsuccessful people is that successful people are willing to do things unsuccessful people are not willing to do. Sometimes success means trying one more time.
- Some of the hardest-working people are paid the lowest wages.
- Not all learning happens in a classroom.

Burning Questions

- Have you learned any lessons from hard, sometimes humbling jobs?
- Are you willing to put the hard work in to get what you want out of life?
- What are some ways you've learned to work smarter, not just harder?
- What do you take away from the almond orchard?

4
MATURITY

High School and Hot Rods

Maturity: *the date specified in a note or bond on which the debt is due and payable.*

When I started high school, I had already bought my first dirt bike and my first car, which I purchased when I was fourteen years old, knowing it wasn't going to be a car for the road. I bought that car specifically because we had pulled the orchard, and I could drive it around the orchard, work on it, and tinker with it. My dad's good friend and CPA[7] Bob Gustafson, came out and helped

---

7 CPA: Certified Public Accountant, a licensed accountant who is involved in accounting tasks, such as producing reports that accurately reflect the business dealings of the companies and individuals for which they work. They are also involved in tax reporting and filing for both individuals and businesses.

me rebuild the carburetor, and I really started to learn the mechanics of the internal combustion engine.

Remember, this all came from working in the orchard, earning and investing the money I earned. I had bought those things for myself, which meant I took better care of them than my friends did with their cars and similar big-ticket items. It adds a level of respect, I think, having skin in the game and buying something yourself. This all helped teach me responsibility. If I wanted to modify things, for example, I paid for it and did the work myself. I put a bigger gas tank on my dirt bike, and, again, that came out of my funds. These kinds of expenses taught me that owning things means also having to take care of them and that the expense of many things doesn't stop with a purchase.

At the beginning of high school, I got more involved in mechanical work. I bought my first truck at sixteen, and it was a stick shift. I had driven the tractor, which was also a stick shift but clearly much different from a car. So my first on-road stick shift experience was driving my truck that I had just purchased in Redding back home, which is about an hour-and-a-half drive.

But again, I put my own money into that vehicle. I loved that truck. I took care of it. I upgraded it. I cared for that vehicle on a much higher level than my friends who were all given vehicles. I had a friend who got a car that he raced around and crashed multiple times. And when he did, his response was "My parents will take care of it." I saw the difference between his mindset and my own, which was "This is mine, and I need to take care of it myself." My parents had given me something better than free cars or even money; they helped me invest in character and mindset, which, in my experience, are worth even more than money or success.

In high school, I also started working in the welding shop. I welded a full roll cage onto one of my dad's trucks, a kind of rock crawler truck, which was fun. At that same time, I started working an unpaid internship with a local hot rod shop called Pettersen Motorsports. The owner taught me a lot about working on vehicles.

I remember one night at the shop, later in the evening, when we had just finished getting a Mustang put back together. It was a 1960s Mustang, a '67 or so, a beautiful car. As we were putting the top of the carburetor back on, a washer was dropped down into it . . . and the washer went through it into the motor. Luckily it didn't do damage because we shut the car off as soon as it fell in, but we had to pull that whole engine apart and put it all back together that night because the client was picking it up the next day.

That was another one of those lessons in following through with commitments. The owner had made a commitment to the client. The client was going to pick up the car the next day, and he would be driving it a long distance. The bottom line was that the owner made sure he followed through with that commitment, and we got that Mustang put back together and ready for the client on time.

Because of my experiences at the shop, when I was given the opportunity in my senior year of high school, I was able to go out and work on a race car at Butte College. It was a class, but because of my connection with the motorsports store, I was able to audit the class and help work on the race car. It was really cool. It was my first experience in the college realm, which led me to think working on race cars was the way I wanted to go. I liked the hot rod shop, and I loved welding. I wanted to combine the two and have my own custom hot rod shop. That was my plan coming out of high school; I was going to learn how to do all the mechanical work and open up my own shop.

High school was also when I met my wife, Michelle. In my junior year, Michelle and I started hanging out and talking, and senior year we went to prom together as friends. She was close friends with one of my classmates. We had smaller learning communities within our high school, and I was in a video production group. We learned how to create movies, do sound voiceovers, all of those sorts of things, and she was in another small learning community that was a little more relaxed. Because of that, she spent a significant amount of time in our class, and that's where I got to know her. We hung out with friends, but we didn't really start spending time together outside the classroom until college.

Speaking of college, for much of high school, my grades weren't exactly great. In fact, they were pretty bad because I wasn't what you would call an "engaged" student. I found most of the material boring, so I did the bare minimum in most of my classes. My high school counselor actually told me when we were preparing to apply to colleges that "the college path isn't for everyone" and that I might want to consider a different path. However, once I was able to dig into material I was excited to learn, things changed. I wound up earning great grades and did very well in college. My high school teachers might be shocked if they knew I later became the assistant superintendent of a school district.

As high school came to a close, a lot of my focus and planning was related to the hot rod idea. My dad told me, "You can do whatever you want to do with your life, but if you want to open up your own hot rod shop, that means you're going to own your own business. If you're going to own a business, you need to have some background in business. So you need to take business courses and get your introduction to the business world." As a result, even though I had promised myself I'd never have a desk job or go into accounting or finance, I started working toward my business degree at the junior college on his recommendation. That was when I took my first accounting course.

Learning Lessons

- Taking responsibility gives you an appreciation for what you have and leads to wiser decisions.
- Ownership makes you take better care of what you invest in and produces more value in the long run.
- Character, even more than material objects, is extremely valuable and worth investing in.
- When we're young, we have unlimited opportunities, but we may not know they exist. As we grow and explore, we find more of these opportunities.
- Many of us want to leave a legacy. Legacies are not necessarily financial. The most important legacies are the things we teach others and the ways we improve their lives.

Burning Questions

- How has ownership changed the way you approach the things you have?
- What is something you took responsibility for that changed your life?
- What is one valuable skill you've picked up along the way and still use today, maybe in a completely different field than you set out for?
- Who spent the time and effort to teach and mentor you? Have you thanked them? Who are you teaching and mentoring?

5
VALUATION

Accounting for Beginners

Valuation: *an estimate of the value or worth of a company; the price investors assign to an individual stock.*

My first accounting course was called Accounting for Beginners. That was where I met LaRee Hartman. She did the impossible: She made accounting fun. Because of her class, I found out that I was very good at it and understood it on a pretty deep level.

LaRee explained these unfamiliar accounting concepts with an energy that I've never seen anybody have for accounting, or any other subject, really. She was up in front of the class, arms waving, as she talked about each new concept, and as she finished a concept, she always turned to the class and said, "Isn't this fun?"

Having a great teacher for my first accounting class really changed my path from hot rods to accounting. It was during that time that I learned something important: You might have a plan for your life, but things don't always go according to your plan. You need to be able to adapt and react to unforeseen events, adjust your expectations as you encounter new information, and realize there's a bigger force shaping your life than just you and your plans.

Having an amazing teacher like LaRee, who made seemingly boring things fun, also taught me something. She put so much energy into the class that she actually got us excited about accounting, and it showed me how much having passion and putting your whole heart into something can positively affect other people, even change their lives for good.

This experience led me into the next accounting class, a financial accounting course, and then managerial accounting. LaRee was my instructor for that course as well. Since I had done so well in her classes, by that time we both knew I wasn't an average accounting student. She asked me to tutor other students. That became one of my jobs as I worked my way through college. It probably helped me as much, if not more, than it helped the other students. Because my brain tends to go from A to D and skip steps B and C, it helped me to have to explain the concepts and strategies to someone else who didn't understand accounting as easily as I did. I knew the answers intuitively. When I was working with these students, they had to slow me down and say, "How did you get there?"

I'd look at the other student as if to say, "It's obvious that's what the answer is." I had to retrain my brain to think, *Okay, what were the steps I took to get there?* Learning those steps and having to explain them to someone else drilled the concepts into my brain at an even deeper level and gave me a much better foundation than I would have otherwise had. I also had to learn that in order to explain complicated things to people, I had to understand *why* the answer was what it was. Today I try to use the same philosophy because my job is not just to do the investing for my clients, but also to educate them through the process and help them to understand the why.

As I got deeper into accounting, I found it more and more interesting because I got to learn about how financials, balance sheets, income statements, and all of those things work within a company. I also learned more than just how they work for the company—there was also how you can *make* them work for the company, how much leeway companies really have in adjusting their accounting processes, and how that can affect the way recording happens. This was more than just a boring world of black-and-white math; it was a creative world as well. That was one of the things I really enjoyed about accounting as I went deeper. There wasn't necessarily one correct answer, but multiple correct answers. There might be a *better* answer, but there wasn't only one correct answer.

That idea also eventually tied into finance, the idea that there are a lot of different ways to invest. There might be better ways than others, but having the ability to look at many options is really important. A lot of gurus out there say, "Don't work with a financial advisor. Get the S&P 500.[8] Buy those funds." Sometimes that can be just fine, and if you're a perfect investor, you buy and hold and don't panic. When the index goes down, you'll probably be okay.

What most people don't realize, though, is that the S&P 500, where we currently sit today, is a market cap–weighted index.[9] Thirty percent of it is allocated to seven stocks. This leads to high concentration. High concentration in only a few stocks can lead to high risk and volatility. The bottom half, the bottom 250 stocks, make

8   Note: Indices are unmanaged and investors cannot invest directly in an index. S&P 500: the Standard & Poor's index is a broad-based measurement of changes in stock market conditions based on the average performance of 500 widely held common stocks known as the Standard & Poor's 500.
9   Market cap–weighted: a stock market index whose components are weighted according to the total market value of their outstanding shares.

up only 14 percent of the S&P 500. So people think they're well diversified and own 500 different stocks, and they do, but they're very, very heavily invested in a select few. This strategy may not align with the risk tolerance or goals that many investors have.

In contrast, financial advisors have access to a lot of different tools, including many that other people don't. There are ways to invest in the S&P 500, but it can be done better than a simple index fund. This can allow the investment to more closely align with an individual's risk tolerance. There are ways to direct-index[10] individual stocks in your account, which can allow for tax loss harvesting. There are ways to build in protections on the downside. There are many different ways to find the right investment for you. It really depends on the person and their risk tolerance, goals, and time horizons.

That's where adjustments come in. As someone with a background in accounting, I can look and say, "What does this person really need?" Then I can adjust my model and my philosophy to better fit their needs. You see, just like with hot rods, accounting and financial management involve a huge variety of tools. There are lots of tools for unique situations and needs, and having the right tool for the job at hand makes all the difference.

---

10 Direct-index: an approach to index investing that involves buying the individual stocks that make up an index in the same weights as the index. This is in contrast to buying an index mutual fund or index exchange-traded fund (index ETF) that tracks the index.

Remember that I was a young person with a lot of "nevers." I knew, coming out of high school, that I never wanted to have a boring desk job, and when most people think of boring desk jobs, it doesn't get a whole lot more boring than accounting. I took that first accounting class knowing I never wanted to be an accountant. Then, when I found out I liked it, I eventually decided to change my path. I learned to start holding my nevers a bit more loosely.

Another important part of my life didn't go according to plan. In my grand scheme, my life was supposed to follow a certain order: I would get married and have kids at age thirty-five, when I was already successful. I would be set up financially before I had kids, even before I got married. That's not exactly how it played out in reality, though.

My wife Michelle and I were friends back in high school. We went to the prom together, but not romantically, just as friends. Then later, throughout junior college, we hung out a lot more, and before junior college was over, I had decided I wanted to date her. The relationship grew to the point that I knew I wanted to be more than friends, and thankfully she felt the same. Things got more and more serious, and eventually we ended up getting married. When we were in junior college, we decided to take a big trip together when we finished our first degrees. We talked about taking a semester off to go to Europe. But as we started budgeting for everything and really looked at the numbers, we realized we could take a much longer trip if we traveled across the United States, especially if we drove.

While I was tutoring at Butte College, doing my first accounting degree, I bought my dream car. It was an all-wheel-drive sports car, a Subaru WRX, with over three hundred horsepower to the wheels. It was stage three, turbocharged, and a lot of fun to drive. It went zero to sixty in about four seconds; it was a really, really fun car. And even though I loved that car, I knew selling it was the best way to fund our big trip. I sold my dream car and bought a used 1979 Toyota motor home.

Learning Lessons

- When you're passionate about what you do, other people will be attracted to it.
- Keep an open mind because your plans won't always go the way you think they will. Plans change, sometimes for the better.
- There's usually more than one right answer when it comes to accounting and finance, although there is such a thing as a *better* answer.

- Learn the "why" of something, and teach others the why as well, and you'll both understand it at a deeper level.
- Invest in a good education that teaches you valuable and marketable skills.
- Sometimes you learn the most when you least expect it.

Burning Questions

- What is your passion? How have you seen other people respond to the way you approach it?
- Have you ever had to change your plans and it worked out for the better?
- What problems in your life might have more than one right answer?

6
RISK TOLERANCE

Camping Across the Country

Risk tolerance: *the degree to which you can tolerate volatility in your investment values.*

The Toyota motor home we bought was no larger than eighteen feet bumper to bumper and cost less than four thousand dollars all in. We drove it across most of the United States over the course of seven months. We had decided to take a year off college and drove it across most of the United States over the course of seven months.

We started in California and drove north. We went up into the Seattle area, to the north end of Washington, zigzagged across the top of the United States, and drove all the way into Maine. We went down into West Virginia, circled back up to Washington, DC, then headed back up into the Northeast for the holidays. We spent Christmas and New Year's Eve that year in New York City, then drove the motor home all the way down to Florida. Finally, we drove across the bottom of the United States. We missed some of the belt states in the middle, but we hit all the states around the edges of the country. We gave ourselves a limit because we knew we were on a budget. We wouldn't drive any more than a hundred miles on any given day. This had the added benefit of forcing us to enjoy each destination and do more exploring. For us, it really was about the journey.

We went from Walmart parking lot to Walmart parking lot because they allowed boondocking, so we could stay there most nights. We would go do our grocery shopping, stay the night, then move on to the next Walmart. That way, the whole trip cost us around fourteen thousand dollars for most of a year. Don't get me wrong; there were a lot of peanut butter and jelly sandwiches, and we ate a ton of eggs. However, we were so busy seeing the country that we often ate only once a day, when we arrived at the next Walmart. At the end of the day, we went into the store and bought a dozen eggs. We ate six eggs each with a couple of pieces of toast, and that was our meal for the day. There was just so much to do.

I remember visiting New York City, and we were actually staying in a hotel, which was a Christmas gift from my parents. The hotel was in New Jersey and we took the hotel shuttle that was available because it was an airport hotel. So we got up in the morning, took the hotel shuttle to the airport, then took the airport trains in to the city to explore. And then, in reverse order on the way back, we would come back to the airport and take the hotel shuttle back to the hotel. I remember getting back one night about midnight. We were both starving, and we realized that we just went the whole day exploring New York City and never once ate because we were so busy having fun.

While we were in New York, we took bus tours to see the holiday lights, saw a Broadway play, went to the famous sites, and attended the New Year's Eve party at Dave and Buster's. We didn't necessarily plan for all of this at the outset of our trip, but we were able to adjust our schedule as we went along to hit these special places on particular dates, and it made the trip that much more special.

The things we were able to do on this road trip, and the timing of them, are things that most people won't get to do in a lifetime. It was all possible because we did the planning it took to be spontaneous. We spent a lot of time traveling across the United States. We went into

Yellowstone. I have family members who own a cabin at a lake on the north side of the park, so we stayed there for a week. We also camped inside Yellowstone, and a moose walked literally inches from our motor home while we sat inside and watched it go by.

We explored Mount Rushmore. We visited friends my wife had met through mission trips at church while we were in Milwaukee. I blew two tires just outside Chicago; that was an adventure in and of itself. We flew from Chicago to Saskatchewan for a family wedding. My grandmother prompted that. She called us, and paid for the flight so we could join the family wedding.

My mom flew from California to Chicago, and we ate at a restaurant called Texas de Brazil. It was very fun. They bring all this meat around, and after being on the road at that point for several months, the ability to eat as much good meat as we wanted was incredible. We definitely took advantage of that. That day, I ate until I thought I was going to explode.

We went into Detroit and saw how run down the city had become at the time, but we did visit some incredible art museums there. In Maine, we saw the Portland Pirates, a minor league hockey team, play. We were students and had our college IDs, so we were able to get seats right on the glass for a cheap price. We spent Halloween in Salem, Massachusetts, which has an incredible festival. I remember walking through the downtown area, and everybody was in costume. From there we went into Washington, DC, toured the White House, and explored the Smithsonian museums. These museums are free to visit, which is incredible. You could spend days experiencing each one. The fact that we have that available to us, free of charge as Americans, is remarkable.

When we were in Boston, we stayed with a friend. We were just blocks from Harvard because our friend was attending school there at the time. We got the opportunity to go onto the Harvard campus and into the library because he was allowed to bring one guest with him at a time. It was amazing.

Again, we took this huge chance, pausing our schooling and traveling across the country in this little motor home on our own, but the reward was incredible. Remember, it takes risk to get reward, when you're willing to take the risk and you're actually prepared. In our case, we prepared well, in many ways indirectly. The experiences I'd had throughout my lifetime prepared me for taking that risk and being able to experience the rewards. Not only will I never forget that trip, but it included experiences that most people will never get to have because it's a risk that most people never take.

Preparation is important if you're going to take risks, though. For instance, my background working on cars and fixing things came in handy a few times during the trip. When we were in the Minneapolis area, we ended up in a parking spot on the side of the street near St. Paul's Cathedral, and we were stuck because my clutch slave cylinder went out. I walked a couple of miles to the local O'Reilly Auto Parts, and bought a new slave cylinder. Then I crawled under the motor home, right there on the street, changed out the cylinder, and we kept going. It's obviously not something we planned for, but it was possible because I had taken the time to learn about auto mechanics. That also gave me the confidence to buy that old motor home in the first place knowing that if something went wrong, I could fix it.

Again, my first on-road vehicle had been a Toyota pickup truck, so I had experience working on that vehicle that allowed me to work on my Toyota motor home. When we got to Florida, for example, we parked at my uncle's house because I had to replace my muffler. In his driveway. He helped me to get it done, and we were able to continue on our adventure.

By the end of the trip, we were excited to get back to regular life. We had been on the road for six and a half months, and we changed one of our rules from the beginning of the trip: the limit of one hundred miles a day. That had been our way of ensuring that we took our time, but when we left Florida, and specifically after we went to New Orleans, we realized there wasn't a whole lot in Texas that we wanted to see. That was the point when we allowed ourselves to really drive (relatively speaking). We still took the back highways as we had done all the way along our trip because our motor home did really well at about forty-five miles an hour. As we went back across the country, we did make a few more important stops. For example, we obviously stopped at the Grand Canyon, because how could you not?

From there, though, we were on our way. We had already talked to my sister-in-law and her husband in San Clemente, where my brother-in-law was stationed. He was in the Marines and and he was being deployed, but my sister-in-law was in nursing school, and they had a young baby, so we made it there in time for her to start her next semester. We parked our motor home down the street from their house and spent about three months there, helping her with the child care. It was kind of a capstone to our trip, in a way.

This trip was a year of great experiences. We spent about seven months in the motor home, about three months in San Clemente, and a few weeks in Santa Cruz with one of my wife's cousins. We saw family and friends all around the nation. We stayed with my great-uncle in

Florida. We stayed at my aunt and uncle's house in Montana. In Idaho, they had a cabin, so we stayed there. We stayed with friends in Milwaukee and a church friend in Boston. But we also had a whole lot of nights at Walmart.

And that was all before senior college. Even though a lot of financial advisors will tell you, "Don't take a gap year," because people are afraid you might not go back and finish school, I say the exact opposite. I think you should take the opportunity when you're young to do things you won't have the time or ability to do when you're older, as long as you've got a plan.

Learning Lessons

- Don't be afraid to take risks as long as you've thought them through and have some kind of plan. We often learn more from failure than from success.
- When seeking opportunities, evaluate both the risk and the potential reward. Ask yourself, if this doesn't work out, what's the worst that can happen? If that outcome is acceptable and the potential reward outweighs the risk, take the risk.
- The biggest risk of failure is to be afraid to follow your dreams. Don't end up looking back on what could have been if you had just tried.

- Invest in skills that might come in handy later in life, especially if you find yourself on an adventure.
- There's no replacement for friends and family you can trust (and maybe visit from time to time).
- Be flexible with your rules, limits, and plans; you'll want to adjust them from time to time to take advantage of new opportunities.

Burning Questions

- What risks have you taken in your life, and what experiences came from them?
- Are there future adventures you want to plan for?
- Who are the people in your life that you want to see, spend more time with, and have more memorable experiences with? What will it take to actually make it happen?

1
SOCIAL BONDS

Marriage and Managing

Social bond: *a bond instrument in which the proceeds will be applied exclusively to finance or refinance, in part or in full, new and/or existing eligible social projects.*

After the year of our epic cross-country trip, Michelle and I knew two things: first, that we could face anything together, and second, that we needed to finish college.

When we first started spending a lot of time together, Michelle had never been to Disneyland. Early in our relationship, we took a trip there together. It was an amazing experience, something we'll always remember.

We went a few more times after that, and it became a special place to us.

About a year after our epic trip, I was ready to propose. I had called ahead, planned, and asked about this special spot in Disneyland. I knew that was where I wanted to do it. I let Disney know when we were going to be there, and they reserved this spot for us in the park.

That night we went to see the fireworks show, and I told her that they were going to let us take a picture because they had the castle all roped off. So we went out and they let us through the rope to take our picture. She was looking at the castle, and then she turned around to look at the photographer. And there I was, down on one knee, in front of thousands of people ready to watch the fireworks. It was really a special moment. And after she said yes, of course, there was cheering and clapping all around us.

That kind of public display was not something I was naturally comfortable with, but I knew I wanted to do it for her. Sometimes you have to step out of your comfort zone to show the people you love how much they mean to you.

Once we were engaged, we started planning and preparing for the wedding as a team. We knew that we didn't want to pay a huge amount for some random wedding venue. Especially because my parents had the orchard, and their house was beautiful. But this venue needed some work. The yard had been in poor repair since I moved out, so we spent the whole summer before we got married digging and cutting and getting everything ready.

We took down bushes and trees, planted flowers, and removed some of my old dirt bike jumps that were out in the backyard. There was a lot of leveling to do. My younger cousin joined us working in the summer heat. The three of us were out there day after day, sweating, moving somewhere close to twenty trailer loads of dirt out of that yard. Sometimes we were out there in hundred-degree heat, swinging pickaxes and shoveling dirt into the trailer and then taking it across the orchard and putting it in the big dirt pile on the other side. We got everything looking really good.

The wedding day was great. Everything went the way we wanted it to, and the venue was beautiful. Not only did we do all the landscaping, but we were able to use my parents' big red barn. That had been the second part of the cleanup, clearing the barn out and getting rid of a lot of junk.

We spent weeks preparing that barn for our dance floor. My dad had a small eight-foot aluminum boat that we cleaned up and filled with drinks and ice. We had a DJ, and we had a taco truck come and cater our meal. This wedding took us a lot of time and effort, but it only cost us about $5,000. And it was everything we had hoped it would be.

We had friends who had a larger wedding in the Bay Area, and it cost about $60,000. Their wedding was two weeks after ours. It was at a beautiful country club with a great dinner, and it really was an incredible event. It was everything they had dreamed of for their wedding. Our wedding was exactly what we wanted, but we were able to arrange it in such a way that the budget was about a tenth of what a wedding like that typically costs.

For my friends, their wedding was worth the cost. For me, though, an amazing event like that is not where I prefer to put my money. Each person has different values and resources, and it's important to keep that in mind. However, if a large or expensive wedding isn't your highest priority, saving on the cost of an event like that can make a big difference in the long run. A more modest wedding budget, say, $20,000, could allow you to invest the other $40,000. If that amount earns just 7 percent per year, it could compound to $559,793 over forty years. If it earns 9 percent, it could compound to $1,152,639![11]

As far as our wedding was concerned, all that hard work saved us an incredible amount of money, but it also had the added benefit of slimming me down. I was in the

---

11   This is a mathematical example of the concept of compounding only. It does not represent actual investing. Past performance is never indicative of future results.

best shape of my life from doing all that yard work. We'll never forget that day because it was everything we wanted it to be. Again, it took planning, effort, and discomfort at times, but it brought great rewards.

We got engaged, prepared for the wedding, and got married, all while working and going to school. When I proposed, I was already working outside my comfort zone managing an apartment complex. My grandparents had these apartments that my grandpa had built years before when they owned a construction company. I was somewhat familiar with their way of managing these apartments, and I had helped with the bookkeeping occasionally.

While I was searching for a job after coming back from our big road trip, I saw a notice for an apartment manager, and the job included rent and a small stipend. I didn't feel completely qualified for it, but again, I stepped outside my comfort zone and applied anyway. Within hours of interviewing for the job, I accepted the job offer. So I managed a fifty-four-unit apartment complex starting just after the trip, through becoming engaged and then married, and until I finished college. All in all, I managed those apartments for about two and a half years.

While I was there, my responsibilities grew. I began doing maintenance during the summer, so I was part of the maintenance team for move-outs. Over time, I took over cleaning, the laundry room, and some other things, which built my stipend up. I also continued to do some tutoring privately and served as a test proctor at our state college to earn some extra income. I was definitely busy, as I was doing all of that on top of taking fifteen units each semester.

Apartment management was a great job that taught me a lot about responsibility. I was the person who knocked on doors and told people when they were being too loud or when rent was overdue. I handled all those kinds of things. That taught me a lot about how to handle people and deal with different personalities.

During my career, I've had the opportunity to hire (or help hire) quite a few employees. You may be surprised to learn it's not typically the 4.0 students who are the most successful. Particularly in stressful environments such as a CPA firm, where there are strict deadlines and high volumes of work. The hires who tended to be the most successful were usually good students who earned a 3.0–3.5 GPA while having a full courseload (twelve semester units or more) and holding a part-time job. My experience has taught me that those students had to learn how to prioritize their work, how to juggle the responsibilities of a job with designated hours *and* get their school work done. These same students also typically graduated with less debt and had real work experience that made them more attractive candidates.

Michelle was also in school at the time, and she worked nights as a caretaker, however, she was a bit more intensely focused on school than I was, as she was taking eighteen units and her courses were more writing intensive. We both worked very hard through college, taking more courses than typical students.

When I was finishing college, I knew I needed 150 units to become a CPA. As I was getting ready to graduate, I was already far past what I needed, but I decided to take my last few classes and get a minor in management. At the time, I didn't really have a true picture of the accounting landscape. I knew I was going into accounting, but I didn't know exactly what that meant. I never wanted to work in public accounting, though, because that was too boring. Another never. I had made up my mind to go into accounting, work my way up the ranks, and eventually become a CFO (chief financial officer).

I didn't want to be the standard "boring" public accountant—that is, until my dad introduced me to someone he knew through his business relationships. I called this gentleman, a CPA with a large regional accounting firm named Tadd, because my dad said, "I told him about you, and he really wants to talk." So I talked to him for a while and enjoyed our conversation. I then met him at one of our Beta Alpha Psi meetings, which was the accounting club. I was introduced to him and another gentleman named David, who was the HR representative for the same accounting firm. There were four locations, and the company had about a hundred staff members. I had never thought I would work for a company like that, but I liked these guys. They were both really relatable.

David had an ability to bring you in and make you feel welcome. He and Tadd were great guys to spend time with. They really made an impression on me. At that point, I decided that if they were in public accounting, I could see myself doing it too. They definitely broke the stereotype of the boring accountant.

David and Tadd got me on the interview list. I went and interviewed with the company about two weeks later, and I was offered a position. I graduated in December, and on January 12, I began my accounting career.

Learning Lessons

- Getting out of your comfort zone, like I did when I proposed to my wife, can bring lasting benefits.
- Weddings and other celebrations cost more than you think they do and can have significant financial impacts on your future.
- Opportunities exist for those who are willing to find and pursue them.
- Working through college rather than taking out student loans helps build the kind of skills and character that translate into career success and personal growth.
- Learning how to deal with people, like I did while managing an apartment complex, is one of the most valuable skills you can invest in.
- Life experience is often a great teacher.

Burning Questions

- Have you ever done something outside your comfort zone that had significant benefits in your life?
- What kinds of jobs have taught you the most valuable lessons in your own life?

8
VALUE INVESTING

Long Days and Short Nights

Value investing: *a strategy in which investors purchase equity securities that they believe are selling below their estimated true value. The investor can profit by buying these securities, then selling them once they appreciate to their real value.*

I knew that by going into public accounting, I was crossing another one of my "nevers" off the list. What I didn't anticipate was how intense it would be. As we went into that first tax season, having shown up on January 12, one of the first questions I had after our orientation was "Where is Tadd's office?" I wanted to say hi.

But the people in charge looked at me and said, "Tadd's not here anymore."

I was shocked. The person I had decided to go work with, the one who had helped me see myself in the company in the first place, wasn't there just a few weeks later. Fortunately David was still there, and I enjoyed his company, so that was something.

In any case, I got started and signed an agreement with the regional accounting firm. With the merger that had just happened, the firm became much bigger, and a lot of the management shifted away from local control, making it a really difficult time for the company.

For my first three months or so, we probably averaged one person leaving the company per week. Eventually, the culture became toxic. Management began sending instructions to employees not to announce when they were leaving anymore. This was because it was causing people to panic. The work still had to get done, but we had fewer bodies to do it. So, although they had estimated that my wages and overtime during tax season would come out to about $51,000 total, that first year I made over $60,000 and worked over 2,700 hours. That's an average of about fifty-two hours a week for every week of the year.

I felt the time crunch even more keenly because shortly after tax season, we had our first child. Lincoln was born in May of that year, and I had started at the company in January. I was definitely in the thick of it. Not only that, but I knew I needed to obtain my CPA. That meant right after tax season ended, after a mandatory minimum of sixty-five hours a week (and I was doing more than that), I began studying. That would be my main focus. I was on a deadline to obtain my CPA. Obviously, I did take some time off to be with my family when my son was born, but right after that, I was studying and working, working and studying.

I remember getting up at four o'clock in the morning, studying until about seven, getting ready and going to work. After work, I would spend a couple of hours with my family before we put Lincoln to bed, and then study again before I went to bed. I would study until ten or eleven o'clock at night and then be up again at four o'clock studying. I did that for about a year and a half, which is how long it took me to finish all the examinations. I think it goes without saying this would not have been possible without the support of my beautiful wife.

I did take breaks for my exams, and I tried to time them with our busy seasons. In our slower seasons, which were by no means actually slow, I would focus on my studies and try to get an exam done. During the busy season, I just didn't have time to study. But the work did help. It's kind of funny when you're taking these exams because there's the exam, there is theory, and then there's practice. The exams are all based on theory, so the longer you work in the industry, the harder it becomes to pass exams because theory turns into practice. The two are not necessarily the same.

I think this applies well to what we do at my firm now because there's a theory of how you should invest and then there's the actual practice. In practice, things work differently. So what I do for my clients may not be exactly what the theory or the book says to do because I take the practical into account as well. In practice and in life application, I've found that often things work differently from the way the books say they do. For example, people say annuities[12] are tax efficient. In some ways they're correct, but in a lot of other ways, they're not. This is because when you take an annuity, you do get tax deferral. So you don't have to pay taxes on it while it's growing. But when you take the money out, annuity income is taxed as ordinary income. Now, when you have appreciation with stocks,[13] bonds[14] (bond interest is typically taxed at ordinary income rates, but appreciation can

---

12 Annuity: a financial product that pays out a fixed stream of payments to an individual, primarily used as an income stream for retirees.

13 Stock: A long-term, growth-oriented investment representing ownership in a company; also known as an *equity*.

14 Bond: a form of loan or IOU issued by a corporation, a municipality, or the US government. The issuer promises to repay the investor the full amount of the loan on a specific date and to pay a specified rate of return for the use of the money at specific time intervals.

get long-term capital gains[15] treatment), mutual funds,[16] or ETFs,[17] you pay long-term capital gains tax. These are taxed at a preferential rate. So if the goal is to take money out at retirement, I'd rather take it out and pay the long-term capital gains rate than pay ordinary income tax rates. Theory versus practice. For a lot of people, the difference between the two rates is 5 percent or more, which is significant. For those in a lower tax bracket, the long-term capital gains and qualified dividends can be taxed at a 0 percent tax rate.

Sometimes blending all of it makes sense. I have a fairly high income compared to a lot of Americans; however, I can still make Roth IRA[18] contributions, and I do that because I want to have different pots of money I can draw from. I have my Roth money, which will be tax-free; I have my traditional retirement money, which I know I'll be taxed on when I withdraw it; and then I also do non-qualified investing.[19] And that gives me options.

Investing is kind of like a puzzle, and everybody's puzzle looks different. What might be the right answer

15 Long-term capital gains: earnings derived from assets that are held for more than one year before they are sold.
16 Mutual fund: a fund operated by an investment company that raises money from shareholders and invests it in stocks, bonds, options, commodities or money market securities.
17 ETF: exchange-traded fund, a type of pooled investment security that operates much like a mutual fund.
18 Roth IRA: an individual retirement account (IRA) funded with after-tax dollars, making qualified distributions tax-free.
19 Non-qualified investment: an investment that does not qualify for any level of tax-deferred or tax-exempt status. Investments of this sort are made with after-tax money.

for one person may not be best for another person. Everyone's life and situations are different. I enjoy putting the puzzle pieces together to help design a customized plan to each person's situation and needs.

In my life, the first year of my career, we bought our first house in Chico. We had been able to save a lot, and then I had the blessing of help from my parents. It was a small house on a big lot right next door to a big church, so we had great neighbors. It got a little busy on Sundays, but other than that, it was pretty quiet. It was a great launching point, and it was comfortable for us at the time. Homeownership tends to be very important for most investors, as it's the most common way that people in America build wealth.

When I buy a house (we've bought a few now), my rule is that I need to make sure it's somewhere we can be comfortable for a minimum of five years. Even if it's a shorter time frame, we want to have some runway. The plan for that first house was to be there for maybe a couple of years, to launch our family life with it as our starter home. But we could have been comfortable there for longer. Your realtor and lender will typically want you to max out your home-buying budget, but don't do that. It will limit your ability to invest in other ways.

Speaking of real estate agents, I've made solid decisions in my life for the most part, but when we bought that first house, I made somewhat of a rookie mistake. At one open house, we made contact with a realtor who then became "our realtor." She was confident and persuasive, and without knowing better or interviewing other agents, we agreed to work with her. Unfortunately, our realtor made several errors that ended up costing us.

First, she seemed eager to close a deal and didn't seem to negotiate effectively on our behalf. Instead, she was pushing us to make an offer that would be quickly accepted (and, at the time, it wasn't a particularly hot market). Second, she didn't do her homework. We purchased a house that was sold to us as a three-bedroom, one-bathroom home. Later, when we sold the home, we found out the remodel that had added the third bedroom wasn't properly permitted and, due to a water heater placement, it wasn't a legal bedroom. When the time came, we ended up having to sell the house as a two-bedroom, one-bathroom home, which dropped our listing price significantly. Finally, much of the paperwork throughout the escrow process was incorrectly filled out, and I had to ask her several times to correct it. Her comment regarding these corrections was that I must be "very detail-oriented." My opinion is that when it comes to one of the largest purchases of someone's life, the professional guiding them should be "very detail-oriented" as a matter of course.

Years later, when buying and eventually selling our next home, we interviewed several realtors and chose the one we felt was most qualified. We were very happy with our choice in the second round. We had learned that business is business—we had been afraid to hurt our first realtor's feelings by seeking another professional, and so we ended up hurting ourselves financially (we lost $10,000 to $20,000). When making big investments or important decisions, seek the opinion of an expert. They may not necessarily be the first person you meet, but it's important to ensure that the professional you're working with is both competent and determined to pursue your best interest over their own.

After we made our home purchases, we made significant improvements to the homes while we lived in them and later sold them at a profit. This was much less risky than flipping or renting houses. There were no tenants to deal with and no pressure to sell a property quickly because it was sitting vacant and costing money. We were able to improve the houses in ways that made them more livable and more valuable over our time there.

Chico is a great place to live. I had kind of a typical childhood growing up, riding my bike around town with my friends. We would ride through Bidwell Park, the second-longest municipal park in America (Central Park in New York City is the longest). It runs all the way through the center of Chico up into the Sierra Nevada Foothills. Today we live a few blocks from the park, and I can ride my bike from our home to the back door of our offices. I enjoy going to the park with my family because it's a beautiful spot.

As our family grew, it definitely changed some things about life and my perspective on it. I've always had the mentality of "family first," but having kids really drove that home. While I was working my first tax season, I was in the office a lot. And during audit season, I was traveling often. I would leave on Sunday afternoon or evening, and we would often drive a couple of hours away. I would stay the night there all week while I worked and come home Friday afternoon or evening. Then I'd leave again Sunday afternoon. That schedule just wasn't working for me. Being away from my family all the time wasn't something I wanted to maintain long term.

That was what led me to one of my first job changes. I was considering getting out of public accounting and trying to figure out exactly what that would look like, but I wasn't necessarily done with it. I just wanted it to look different.

Another partner was leaving my first firm as I was making the decision to leave, and we had a lot of conversations about it. She encouraged me. Her first comment was "Why don't you go join your dad? You're always talking about money management and investing. You clearly know a lot about it and I think you would be good at it. Why don't you go do that?"

At the time, I had two main reasons. First, I wanted to ensure no one could ever say, "You're only where you are because of your dad." While there's truth in that—he provided me with an incredible foundation and supported me through my education—I wanted to establish my own identity and build my own reputation. Second, his partnership at the time included someone I didn't see myself working with, either then or in the future. I enjoyed researching and discussing investments, but I knew it wasn't the right time to join my dad professionally. Not yet.

While I didn't end up joining my dad just yet, I did find a smaller more family-friendly firm in Chico. My second CPA position was with a great group of people. That same partner was the one who referred me there. At one point she decided to introduce me to someone she had worked with at our firm named Tim Tittle, so she gave him my information. Shortly after that, Tim called me, and we chatted.

He said, "I don't know how it is there today, but I left because of these big issues that I was facing ..." He listed his reasons for leaving, and I couldn't have said it better myself. He must have detailed the top ten issues

I was having with that firm. We definitely saw eye to eye on that.

After we had chatted a little more, I went in for an interview with him and his partner, and I made the decision to go work for their firm. It was a great office full of great people, and it allowed me to continue to grow and see things early in my career that I normally wouldn't have been exposed to. It was a kind of trial by fire. I remember one of the partners at my first firm telling me in my first year, "This is a project we normally wouldn't assign to you until your fourth year, but in this case, because of the way staffing is, you're going to get it now." He told me that it was going to be hard but that it would be a learning experience and he would help me through. So, even early in my career, I had a few things I specialized in, such as doing taxes for rental partnerships and for farmers with a special type of return called an IC-DISC.

I was also on the estate planning team. I helped with estate tax returns and estate planning. Those experiences have been beneficial for where I am today. The knowledge I built there has helped me a lot in understanding people's financial situations and helping them with estate planning and related areas.

When I was sacrificing for the long days and short nights of that part of my career, I always tried to do it in a way that would let me continue to put my family first.

Even though I'm not a morning person, I've had to force myself to become one. When I work extra hours, I tend to get up while everybody else in the family is still sleeping and get my work done so I can spend the evenings with them. This was a big part of what I did in those long days and short nights. That way I could still be with my kids while I was studying and working tax season.

During my time in public accounting practice, I was also doing school audits. They were not my favorite part of the job. I found government accounting boring, so I knew I never wanted to do it—until I decided to transition away from CPA practice. I was tired of having two tax seasons, audit season, a lot of seasonal overtime in the spring, a good amount of seasonal overtime in the fall, and wrap-up at the end of the year. I was looking for a way out.

I didn't know exactly what would happen, but a friend from one of my prior CPA firms sent a job out, and it was for a school district. I was familiar with it, and he said, "You could be a really good fit here. They're looking for somebody with your skill set."

I looked at the job description, and honestly I didn't fit the requirements. I made the phone call anyway. I knew the secretary at the school district, and I called her and said, "I don't meet the requirements here, but I have a good idea of what you're going through. I think I can do it. My background would fit. Do you want me to apply?"

And her answer was, "Please do." So I did.

Learning Lessons

- Learning the theories of a field or area of study, like accounting, is important, but the practice of that discipline is often quite different; you need both theory and practice.
- As your life changes, you might have to make new sacrifices and changes in perspective to have the life you really want.
- Homeownership is the most common way Americans build wealth; it's worth making sacrifices elsewhere to reap the benefits of homeownership.

Burning Questions

- What's an area of your life where theory and practice don't always work the same way?
- What's one important change in perspective you've had to make as your life has progressed?

9
IMPACT INVESTING

Public Service

Impact investing: *a sustainable investment style that seeks to generate measurable positive social or environmental impact alongside financial return. Investment themes include areas such as affordable housing, education, and health care.*

I applied for the school district position, and I got an interview. The timing wasn't what I would have chosen for myself, but I went, and I connected well with the people at the school district office. I was offered the position. Even before starting the job, I had been reminded of an important lesson: At first glance, something may not look like a fit, but that doesn't mean you shouldn't pursue it at all. I knew that on paper, I wasn't technically qualified. However, as I continued to pursue it, learn more, research, and ask questions, and as we progressed through the interview, it became clear that it really could be a good fit.

In a way, this lesson comes down to taking a leap of faith. Advancements and progress often require it. When I reflect on the various positions I've held, it's been a common theme throughout. It's something I think others can learn from as well, especially young people who are going out and getting their early career jobs. Athletes must constantly push themselves beyond their comfort zone and try new things to reach new levels and set new records. The same is true for the rest of us: Unless we're willing to push ourselves to improve and grow personally and professionally, we risk becoming stagnant, letting others move ahead while we get left behind. Either we're growing and advancing or we're stagnating and declining. If we are getting older and failing to move closer to our goals, those goals are getting harder to achieve every day.

While you may not be a clear fit for an opportunity, many times it's worth putting in the application and trying anyway. If nothing else, it's a great experience to sit down and interview with someone. Requirements in job listings are often just the employer's wish list. The employer may be very willing to hire someone who doesn't meet all the requirements as written but has other skills, qualifications, abilities, and characteristics that make them a better candidate. These abilities may include personality, dedication, enthusiasm, drive, and a great work ethic. In this case, they wanted five years of public school experience, and I didn't have that. I had five years of public accounting experience instead. I had audited schools for five years, and audit season was typically half of each year. So while I wasn't a direct fit, I was still able to get the position. If you don't ask, the answer is always no. If I had just walked away because of that first impression, I never would have had the opportunity to experience and learn so many things that would, in time, be invaluable.

There's also some investment advice here: You may look at an opportunity, a product, or a strategy and say, "That's not for me." But if you have someone you can talk to and get guidance from, like the person I knew in the school system, there may be things about it that you don't fully understand yet. So it might actually be a better fit than you think.

A lot of people out there may tell you that something (a product, investment, strategy) isn't a good fit, and in many cases, they're right. But this is a good reason to have a guide who can understand complex opportunities and explain their benefits clearly. You need to know the risks and benefits of a given opportunity to find the optimum fit for you as an individual. Just as I needed to sit down with a human being and take a closer look to see if I was right for the job, many investors need to sit down with someone who has the facts to make an informed decision about how they want to proceed.

A good example of this is when I sat down with a client about a year ago. This client was getting close to retirement and wanted to know if he would be "okay." Looking at his balances, I brought up an annuity that provided guaranteed income for him and his wife for the rest of their lives.

The client recoiled at the word *annuity*. He said he had always been told annuities were "bad," they were "too expensive," and they weren't good for anyone but the person selling them.

During our conversation about this, I was able to explain that *some* annuities[20] are bad, expensive, and just not worth using. However, in the right situation, some can provide great benefits. In his case, it was the right situation. Due to his age and the market conditions at the time, we were able to guarantee him and his wife over

---

20 Fixed annuities are long-term insurance contracts, and there is a surrender charge imposed generally during the first five to seven years that you own the annuity contract. Indexed annuities are insurance contracts that, depending on the contract, may offer a guaranteed annual interest rate and some participation growth, if any, of a stock market index. Such contracts have substantial variation in terms, costs of guarantees, and features and may cap participation or returns in significant ways. Investors are cautioned to carefully review an indexed annuity for its features, costs, risks, and how the variables are calculated. Any guarantees offered are backed by the financial strength of the insurance company. Surrender charges apply if not held to the end of the term. Withdrawals are taxed as ordinary income and, if taken prior to age fifty-nine and a half, a 10 percent federal tax penalty.

7 percent income on his investment for life. For reference, the typical guidance recommends a maximum safe withdrawal rate of 4 percent, so this was nearly double the safe withdrawal level, and it was guaranteed by a very strong and highly rated company. I explained that it would allow us to cover his base income using only a portion of his funds, so he could hold the remainder of his funds as reserves and continue to grow them. That would enable him to provide for unforeseen expenses and future inflation relief. Not only is this client going to be okay, but he and his wife are set up to *thrive* in retirement.

This relates to another lesson: When you generalize things, you may be setting yourself up for failure, and having an expert who knows the details can really make a difference, particularly in the investing world. A trusted advisor who's extremely knowledgeable, not just about investing in general but about very specific products or investments, can lead you through some of the ambiguity and unreliable information out there.

As I said, there are "bad" annuity options out there. I've helped many clients examine some of these options that other insurance agents or brokers have recommended to them or sold them. In some cases it's very unfortunate because some of them have such high surrender charges that it harms the client and forces them to stay in a subpar investment. This is why it's extremely important to have a highly qualified financial advisor in your corner who is a fiduciary.[21] I take the time and effort to analyze how these investments work. I ask the hard questions to ensure that we're acting in the client's best interest.

Some insurance agents recommend whole-life policies as a good investment. This is often not true. In addition, many of these same insurance agents are not licensed to represent investments. I have the training and licenses for both investments and insurance. There is a small segment of the population that whole-life policies are very helpful for, and they can be a great fit, but for many people, they simply aren't the right option. In my opinion, there are often better ways to invest. Whole-life policies can be useful when utilized for the right purpose, but again, this is only typically the case for a small portion of the population.

When I started the school district position, one of the first phone calls I got was from the county office. The person who oversees my district called and said, "Hey, welcome. I'm glad you're here. Did you know that a couple of months ago, you had negative cash in the bank, and in another month, you're going to have negative cash in the bank again?"

I said, "I had no idea that happened."

---

21 Fiduciary: a person or organization that acts on behalf of another person or persons, putting their clients' interests ahead of their own, with a duty to preserve good faith and trust. Being a fiduciary means being bound both legally and ethically to act in the client's best interest.

He answered that he didn't know what happened either, but somewhere, somehow, the budget was incorrect and it needed to be fixed because we were projected to have negative cash the next month and the following month, which wasn't allowed to happen.

Because of this, I had to make quick changes to save the budget. I also had to prepare a really tough budget, because if I couldn't balance the budget, the state would take over the schools. You don't want the state choosing which things in your school can stay and which ones have to go. They will likely make different decisions than the local community would prefer.

All of this combined to make for a very difficult start to my new position, as you can probably imagine. But at the end of the day, it was my problem to solve, so I opened it up to discussion. I informed my superintendent, who also had no idea about the negative cash situation. It was a total shock to just about everyone.

I informed the school board as well, and from there we started a discussion. Shortly after that, I got the opportunity to sit down at the negotiating table with the educational labor unions. Right before one of my first meetings, my superintendent told me it was a good thing I understood the budget, because when it came to that side of the negotiations, I was on my own.

Because I was the one who had to confront the problem, but I needed the buy-in of others as well, I sat down and explained the budget to our negotiating teams. I explained where we were heading and what needed to change. It wasn't a fun conversation, but it was an important one. And I found that being transparent and putting all my cards on the table really made a difference in how that news was received.

This is a lesson that has been important throughout my career, and it's still important today. Transparency and honesty always need to be brought to the table, and they make it so much easier to gain buy-in. People can accept bad news. They want to know the truth. They want to know you're on their side looking for possible solutions. It's very important for them to know you want to work with them to help and not harm them.

The situation was very difficult. We had to make immediate cuts, and we had to figure out ways to keep the budget under control. I began holding monthly budget meetings and invited not only our school board members but also the teachers' union and the public to learn about the situation and the changes we had to make. In doing that, I took transparency to the next level, which made the conversations behind closed doors much easier.

It turned out that we were able to work together, all of us, which made me much more effective at my job.

Once I opened that door up for everyone and showed them exactly where the money was being spent and where we were heading, we were able to work together to solve the problem of where to make our cuts.

Ultimately, that first year we ended our salary negotiations and the teachers' union took about a 1 percent pay cut for the next year, with an agreement that we would change that if we got more money. The day after we signed that deal, the president of the teachers' union stood up in front of the board, and I was expecting it to be bad news for me. We had just negotiated a pay cut, after all.

But she actually thanked me. She said that my transparency in working with them had been a total change for the district and that they were really excited about the hard work I was putting in to make things better for the future. That's the power of transparency and collaboration.

It was still a tough situation and a hard job, to be honest. Not only did I come into a tough budget situation, but that school district will quite frankly never be one of the rich school districts. It has landlocked eighty-acre parcel minimums, so the funding will always be lower than the other schools have, based on the current funding system. This is because many of the farmers who could afford eighty-acre parcel minimums were earning higher incomes. Current school funding in California is largely based on the income of the population you serve. Schools that serve students in low-income areas receive higher funding via programs like Title I.

Because of that, it's a difficult spot to be in, and we had less help in our district office than in any other district office in the county. That means I traded in the seasonal overtime as a CPA for constant overtime at the district. I ended up averaging seventy-plus-hour weeks throughout the year, coming in early to campus most mornings, just getting things done.

It was a lot of work, but it was also really rewarding because I knew I was doing the public a valuable service. What I did behind the scenes had a direct effect, not just for the people who worked there but for all the kids who were being educated in those schools. It was truly affecting everybody, from the most senior teachers and administrative staff all the way down to the kindergartener who was coming in the door of the elementary school.

Internally, it felt good to know that I was improving things, and that's something I took with me for the future. I love to volunteer. I coached both of my kids' baseball teams. My wife and I both signed up for a spot in the classroom, and every week, one of us was there volunteering our time to help the school. There's a gratification that comes with public service, with knowing you're making a difference and making real connections with other people.

As far as the job was concerned, by the time I had been at the district for over a year, things were improving. I had cleaned up the budget. We had a positive three-year outlook. I was part of issuing the first bond that the district had issued in over thirty years and even got to have my name on the bond offering. That was an experience in and of itself, trying to put together all the paperwork to start the bond and the construction project. We got plans drawn up for replacing portable classrooms that were ten years past the end of their expected lifespan.

A lot had happened in a short time there, but late in the spring, my dad was working on a deal with his business partner. She was going to buy the business from him, and at some point it became clear that deal was not going to happen. They couldn't agree on the terms of the purchase, and eventually he knew he wasn't going to sell to her.

Not selling meant he needed help. He'd had a business partner, a succession plan, and a retirement plan in place for several years that had let him cut back on his time and responsibilities and focus on what he enjoyed the most, which was talking with clients and managing their portfolios. He needed somebody to come in and help run the business, and that was part of our conversation.

My first reaction was to tell him, "You've been working on the deal for the last five years. Make it work. But if you can't make it work, I'll be there for you."

From there, they went through a few more iterations of trying to negotiate a deal, and at the end of the day, they weren't able to make it happen.

I had told the district before all of this that my family would always be my first priority. The decision to leave my position as assistant superintendent wasn't a decision I made because I wanted out of the school district. It was hard work, but I wasn't done in Durham. I wasn't looking to leave. However, when my father needed somebody in his business, I told him I would go, so I did. And ultimately this has been the best transition I ever could have asked for.

Learning Lessons

- Taking a leap of faith to pursue something that might not seem like a perfect fit at first glance can open up new opportunities and potential rewards.
- Not settling for general understanding, but really getting the details and the guidance you need, can change the way you perceive an opportunity.
- Don't close doors without knowing what's behind them. Never say never. Life can be much better than we could have ever imagined.
- You can't change the past, but you can change your future.
- Honesty and transparency, especially about hard things, combined with collaboration can completely transform a situation or relational dynamic.
- Problems are often opportunities in disguise.

Burning Questions

- When was a time that your perspective on a situation or opportunity changed as you learned the details?
- Has there ever been a time when something less than a "perfect fit" ended up being important or rewarding for you?

10

PREFERRED STOCK

Family First

Preferred stock: *a class of stock with a fixed dividend that has preference over a company's common stock in the payment of dividends and the liquidation of assets. There are several kinds of preferred stock, such as adjustable-rate and convertible stocks.*

If you asked any of my coworkers, past or present, they would say I talk about investing all the time. This is what I do for fun. Even in college, I would finish up my studies and scroll on my computer or phone, reading articles and doing research about my own investing (I actually won the investing competition in the investing club in junior college). So when my dad needed help, I transitioned from being an assistant superintendent to talking to my clients and helping them invest. Now, I'm able to be paid for something that before was just a fun hobby. It's one of those situations a lot of people only dream about: "If you enjoy your job, you'll never work a day in your life." I'm one of the lucky few who can say that I truly enjoy my job.

I'm grateful that I get to do what I do partially because, years ago, it was one of my nevers. I had two reasons I thought I'd never go to work for my dad. One was that I didn't want to work with his business partner; I believed it would be a struggle if I did. My second reason was that I wanted to be successful on my own. I didn't want anybody to accuse me of riding his coattails.

In my career leading up to joining my dad, I accomplished that. I went out into the world and worked diligently to become the best I could be in a variety of settings. I became the assistant superintendent of a school district, which is about as high as you can go as an accountant in the school world. I was able to build a name and a solid reputation for myself. Now my dad needed somebody to come in and help him run the business. This was a growing dream and one that I enjoyed talking about. Things fell into place, and I decided to make the jump.

It was, however, another tough start. I've had quite a few tough starts throughout my career, walking into situations where there were plenty of things that needed to be done and not enough hands to do them. I officially joined the company the day after his partner left. Within a week, we found out that another longtime employee was leaving whom we had expected to stay. My dad had worked the previous thirty-plus years without having to do most of his own paperwork because he had assistants who had been with the company for a long time.

Now, it was just the two of us. So we had to figure things out quickly. Between what I had done in the school district and my experience as a CPA, I was prepared to make the transition and figure out what forms to fill out. I learned how to fill them out quickly. Together, we were able to combine our backgrounds and strengths to fill the gaps and create a solid foundation. It was tough, we worked long hours, and did a lot of paperwork.

A little more than a month after I started, I was able to bring on our first employee of the new era. She was really good at the job, but unfortunately she got a job offer that I couldn't beat. I had to be honest about what was best for her, so I told her she had to take it. She was with us for about a month and a half, and we had just hired our first intern right before she left. At that point, it became me, my dad, and an intern.

A lot of work goes into this business. This is particularly true on the regulation and paperwork side of things, but, as a whole, when I get to sit down with my clients and explain their situation to them, I love it. When we start putting together a plan to move them forward, to me, that's fun. I get to do something with passion, and that passion comes through in my conversations. My clients can see it.

This is another area where my previous experience had done a great job preparing me for this position. I had been providing financial advice for years. I provided financial advice in the form of tax advice as a CPA. I also provided financial advice to the school district. Prior to this experience, though, many investment conversations began and ended with me advising them to speak with a financial advisor. The biggest change is that now I am that financial advisor.

My favorite part of this job is that I get to help my clients with their actual lives. I get to be a part of the best and worst times in my clients' lives, which is an amazing position to be in. I get to be there when they change jobs, retire, or hit another major financial milestone and celebrate because they're able to do that. I also get to be there to help them through hard times, like when a loved one passes away. I get to tell them it's going to be okay, we can transition things, and we have a plan. Because of that, it's a job that has a huge impact on my clients, and that is something I don't take lightly. It's something I really love.

Of course I'm paid for it, and it's a great career, but beyond that, it's about helping. I recently had several conversations with different clients who have told me, "If we didn't work with you, I don't know what we would do." Clients who have worked with my dad have said, "If it wasn't for him, I wouldn't have anything." And now, my job is to take that legacy and move it forward. I know that what I do has an impact, not just on the clients I work with today but on the next generation and the generation after that. I have the opportunity to be a part of creating generational wealth, of creating a plan, and building a legacy. I get to help people achieve their goals, their dreams, and other things they may not have thought possible. That's another lesson I've learned from my dad: build things that outlast you.

That's what my dad has built: a practice that's going to outlast his career. My goal is to continue that, to continue to build this practice that will outlast my career. He's worked with families of five generations. I have families that I've now worked with three generations, and I'm excited to move on to four or five generations of their family throughout my career. It's a really rewarding thing when I can go from working with Grandma and Grandpa to Mom and Dad and now the kids, and helping each of those generations plan and set themselves up for success.

We've gone from me, my dad, and an intern in those early days to a solid team today. We have three excellent assistants who have been with us for several years now. I spend less time preparing paperwork these days and more of my time reviewing the paperwork, speaking with clients, and focusing on the investments themselves. Jumping right in and having to do all of those forms really did benefit me, though. I now know exactly what goes into every step of the process and what work has to be done to maintain these accounts. Because of the way things started, I have a familiarity with the whole process that makes me a better boss and a better advisor.

I started learning from my dad as a kid, and I haven't stopped watching him and learning from his example. He's still showing me how to put faith and family first, live on less than I earn, invest for the future, seek professional advice and guidance when needed, and so much more.

I've had the opportunity to work with a lot of different professionals throughout my career. Knowing when to seek professional help is really important. When I'm out of my depth, it makes sense to hire someone who specializes in things I don't know as much about. So I have my team of experts: I have realtors whom I know and trust when it comes to real estate, attorneys whom I know and trust when it comes to legal matters, and various professionals on a team I've built over the years whom I know I can rely on. Even when it comes to marriage and family, acting as a team is critical. I feel like it has become more and more common for families to keep their finances and a lot of other things separate, but I'm the opposite. My wife and I put everything together because we function as a team. We're not two separate people; we're one family.

Teamwork is another thing I first learned from my parents. Without my mom caring for the family, my dad wouldn't have been able to do all he did. It's the same for me and Michelle in our marriage. Without my wife doing all she does with the kids, even homeschooling the kids, I couldn't focus on the work of helping my clients the way I do. In the end, that might be the biggest blessing of all: my business is the family business, and putting family first also allows me to have such an impact on the lives of others.

Learning Lessons

- Having a team, especially one composed of experts in their fields, is crucial when it comes to building anything of value over the long term.
- You are never too young or too old to learn.
- What you did yesterday influences today. What you do today will influence tomorrow.
- There are gifts that come only from the blessing of a multigenerational family.
- When you build things that outlast you, you can have a greater impact on the world than you ever imagined.
- Think about where you are today. If you continue on your current path, where will you be five or ten years from now? If you like the answer, you are probably on the right path. If you don't like the answer, choose a different path.

Burning Questions

- Have you received anything of lasting value from previous generations? What have you done with it?
- Are you building anything that will outlast you, something you can pass down to future generations?

11
DIVIDENDS

A Lasting Impact

Dividends: *a portion of a company's profits distributed to shareholders, often serving as a tangible reward for their investment and a testament to the company's financial health and stability. They represent not just a return on investment, but a symbol of long-term commitment and shared success.*

This book is about creating a lasting impact. I wrote this book to help you pursue your goals and have a lasting impact on the world in your own way. That's what I do every day: I help empower people to have their desired impact on their families, their communities, and ultimately the world. This final chapter is where I'm going to compile and summarize all the life and investing lessons I've mentioned along the way so you have a place to learn more and take your next steps toward your investing goals.

First, I'll summarize the big-picture lessons I've learned and mentioned throughout the book that apply to both life and investing. Then I'll give you the "best of the best" investing advice I've learned and gathered over the years so that you can return to this chapter whenever you need to refresh or update your own investment knowledge.

The Big Picture

As I've said, I've learned a lot in my life so far, from family, friends, coworkers, experts, teachers, and life experiences. These lessons help form a bigger picture of what a good life, built on wisdom and truth, really looks like.

Take Risks While You Can

The best time to do this is usually, but not always, when you are younger and have more time to course-correct. Make sacrifices for the things you really want. Sometimes the best way to be spontaneous is to plan for it in advance. Don't be afraid to take risks as long as you've thought them through and have some kind of plan.

Keep an open mind because your plans won't always go the way you think they will. Be flexible with your rules, limits, and plans; you will want to adjust from time to time to take advantage of new opportunities. Getting out of your comfort zone, like I did when I proposed to my wife, can bring lasting benefits.

Taking a leap of faith to pursue something that at first glance might not seem like a perfect fit can also open up new opportunities and potential rewards. Not settling for general understanding, but really getting the details and seeking the guidance you need, can change the way you perceive an opportunity.

Teach Your Kids About Money Early

Teach them how to save, teach them the power of compound interest, and teach them to live on less than they earn. Try your best not to take on debt. Allow your funds to grow; be patient. Good things take time. Work-life balance helps make life worth living. Your kids are watching and will learn from your integrity. There is no replacement for an integrated life.

Invest in People

Investing in growth stocks is wise, but investing in people is the wisest thing you can do. Lead by example and learn from those beside you; no one is above sweat equity or better than the people working around them. When you're passionate about what you do, other people will be attracted to it.

Learning how to deal with people, like I did while managing an apartment complex, is one of the most valuable skills you can invest in. Honesty and transparency, especially about hard things, combined with collaboration can completely transform a situation or relational dynamic.

There's no replacement for trusted friends and family. There are gifts that come only from the blessing of a multigenerational family. Having a team, especially one composed of experts in their fields, is crucial when it comes to building anything of value over the long term. When you build things that outlast you, you can have a greater impact on the world than you ever imagined.

Invest in Yourself

Taking responsibility gives you an appreciation for what you have and leads to wiser decisions. Ownership makes you take better care of what you invest in and produces more value in the long run. Character, even more than material objects, is extremely valuable and worth investing in.

There is usually more than one right answer when it comes to accounting and finance, but there is such a thing as a better answer. Learn the "why" of something, and teach others the "why" as well, and you will both understand it at a deeper level.

Weddings and other celebrations cost more than you think they do and can have significant financial impacts on your future. Working through college rather than taking out student loans helps build the kinds of skills and character that translate into career success and personal growth. Homeownership is the most common way that Americans build wealth; it is worth making sacrifices elsewhere to reap the benefits of homeownership.

Invest in skills that might come in handy later in life, especially if you find yourself on an adventure. Learning the theories of a field or area of study, like accounting, is important, but the practice of that discipline is often quite different; you need both.

The difference between successful people and unsuccessful people is often that successful people are willing to do things unsuccessful people are not. Sometimes success means trying one more time. Sometimes it means sacrificing or doing hard things early on to make things easier for the future. Besides bringing success, hard work can also teach you what you don't want to do forever. You might find ways to work smarter, not just harder. As your life unfolds, you might have to make new sacrifices and change your perspective to have the life you really want.

These are some of the best and most important things I've learned about life along the way, but I don't want to leave you with just general life advice. I want to leave you with a succinct set of guiding principles and investment tools that you can turn back to time and time again. Think of this next section as a "best of the best" of what I've learned as a wealth manager and investor over the years.

The Best of the Best

I got into this business, like my father before me, to help people. This is why we do what we do, why I wrote this book, and why I'm putting this advice on paper in this final chapter. We are here to help people have better lives. We get to walk through the best and hardest moments of people's lives with them to help them pursue their goals and build a lasting legacy, often for several generations of the same family.

These, are the things we've learned that make the most difference when it comes to investing and building wealth. Keep in mind that every person and every situation are unique, so not every principle or tool in this chapter is the best option for everyone. In other words, think of these as a kind of "greatest hits" of investing.

Stay Consistent

First, don't underestimate the value of consistency. You might not expect it, but in fact a large portion of our wealthiest clients have been schoolteachers and administrators who have never made astronomical salaries. You don't have to have a huge salary to build wealth, but you have to be consistent and intentional. You need to plan, consistently put money into investments, let it grow, and follow good advice.

Start Early

Start investing consistently as early as you can. Ultimately, I'm going to make a custom plan for every client, but it starts with sitting down and asking, "Where are you today?" Then we take an inventory and figure out exactly where they are today, financially speaking. We look at debts and income, and then we turn that conversation to "Where do you want to be?" We use the answer to create a custom plan. It's different for every client, but getting started as early as possible is crucial.

Many clients get similar advice because there are things that work for most people, like investing early and often, but beyond that, we create a customized approach to meet a particular client's risk tolerance, goals, and situation. We take their tax bracket into account so that we can build a plan that is tax efficient for them. We determine whether they need guaranteed income and can take more risk or want less risk. For some people that might mean they have a single account for everything, but other people might have ten or twenty different accounts that all work together.

Use Your Resources

As you work to build your wealth, you want to have every possible tool at your disposal. As an independent financial advisor, I don't have anybody telling me what tools to use. Therefore, I have a world of investment options available. I'm also still a tax accountant, so I have all the tax software and planning tools for that. I'm fully licensed and registered to do commission-based business as well as advisory-based business. I can sell annuities. I can use advisory accounts.

Different tools are better or worse depending on the situation, but also depending on when you are investing. For example, sometimes things like annuities have great rates, and other times they're not a strong option.

All of this makes me a stronger advisor and allows me to be flexible and adaptable to your circumstances and to the market conditions. We can move your money where we believe it will do the best, no matter what the current circumstances are. When a financial advisor is not independent, a lot of these options are off the table. Having all those tools at my disposal makes me a stronger advisor than those who don't have them.

Choose Your Risk Level

No matter your circumstances, you need to decide how much risk you are willing to take on with your investments. A lot of the conversation surrounding risk also involves time, and depending on when you're looking to invest, the risk may look different, but it's also suited to people's particular tolerances. I call this a person's "sleep-at-night factor" because I want my clients to be able to sleep. I don't want them up at night worrying about what's happening in the market or in politics or world events, because I want them to know that we've invested their funds in a way they're comfortable with. If people aren't truly comfortable with their investments, they may panic because of a bad day in the market, withdraw funds at a loss, and cost themselves in a major way.

Warren Buffett said no one is willing to get rich slowly, but ultimately that's what it takes. Time is more valuable than money, and the longer you're willing to be patient, the more time you have for that magic compound interest to work for you. When we talk about compound interest, we use the Rule of 72,[22] which describes how long it takes for your money to double. To use this rule, you divide the number 72 by the expected rate of return. The answer is the number of years it will take to double your money.

Over time, the S&P 500 has averaged about 10 percent a year. That means your money doubles approximately every seven years (72 ÷ 10 = 7.2 years). On the other hand, if you're getting only 7 percent interest, it takes ten years for your money to double (72 ÷ 7 = 10.29 years). That's why when you're younger, you'll want to take more risk, because your money's going to grow more quickly. Ultimately, when you double for the first time, it's not as impressive as when you're two or three or even five times down that doubling trajectory. However, by being patient and allowing the process to take place, you can see wealth really start to grow. It's almost like having little workers who are working for you; you're putting your money to work for you.

---

22 Rule of 72: The rule of 72 is a mathematical concept and does not guarantee investment results nor function as a predictor of how an investment will perform. It is an approximation of the impact of a targeted rate of return. Investments are subject to fluctuating returns, and there is no assurance that any investment will double in value.

Invest in What Matters to You

There are intrinsic and extrinsic benefits to investing in things and people you believe in. You get a good feeling when you invest in what matters to you, but there are other benefits as well. For instance, if you invest in people, you build relationships. Relationships are good in and of themselves, but that network you're building can also be there to support you in a number of ways. When I first went into public accounting, it wasn't necessarily what I knew but whom I knew that helped me succeed. That has continued to be the case in almost every part of my career.

Relationships can make a huge difference in the impact you have. Most of our business is not just people off the street. Our business grows because of referrals, because of the relationships, and the ways we invest our time and energy into the lives of our clients.

Pursue Integrity, Character, and Ethics

If you're working with a financial advisor, there's a high likelihood that that person is working with your life savings. You need to know that they have moral integrity and that you can trust them to act in your best interest. In our case, we're not only legally obligated because we're a fiduciary, but we have a moral obligation long before some of those fiduciary rules come into play. That's how my dad has always operated, and how he built a good reputation, which is something we closely protect. You need to be able to trust the people helping you with your money. If you can't, they won't be able to add the value that a professional advisor can bring to the table.

It's not just your advisor's character that matters, though. Your character matters too. A very calm person will do better than a fearful person in times when the stock market goes down. Some people panic because they act on fear. They don't have that inner sense of confidence and calm that you need to build things over time in this world. Faith translates to people's investments.

Many of our clients are people of faith, and when we talk to them, it's common for them to say, "God has a plan." Often when we're dealing with investment decisions, our clients take time to pray and discern what they believe is the best way forward. They tend to have a level of trust in the process similar to the way they have faith in God. They're willing to trust their advisor and trust that things are going to work out, and that allows them to take wise risks, to do what they think is the most faithful thing and be a good steward.

On the other hand, there are people in this world whose financial house is a house of cards. Sometimes (not always) a person's financial life can be a reflection of the life decisions they've made. For example, we know marriage can be one of the best financial decisions you ever make, and divorce can be one of the worst. Additionally, organized people tend to do better than people who lack organization. People who make compulsive decisions tend to have a harder time saving. It turns out that, in general, having virtues like patience and self-control, being truly present, paying attention to the details, and being humble about what you don't know are things that matter in the life of an investor.

Build a Team

Another key to successful investing that's related to humility is that you need a team. No matter who you are, you need to have a team to support you, each person with their own individual expertise. My expertise happens to be financial and tax-related. I am not, however, an expert in fixing computers. I have limited knowledge there. Because of this, I have an IT expert whom I call when my computer is not working right. I am also not an attorney, which means that if I have a legal issue to look into, I ask my attorney to do that. You want many different tools in your tool chest, and you always want to have the right tool for the job. You don't always want the cheapest tool. You want the tool that is going to bring you the most value. For instance, you can get advice from another financial advisor who may be cheaper than us, but they might not offer the same level of knowledge and expertise. I honestly believe that we bring the most value for what we charge.

Be Flexible

Having patience and a good team around you can help you stay open-minded and flexible when it comes to investing. There are a lot of answers out there, but there's a difference between good answers and better answers. For example, you can invest in the S&P 500, and if you just put your money in, leave it there, and don't panic, you'll probably be okay. However, there are ways to get that kind of performance while taking a lot less risk. A lot of people say active funds don't beat the index over the long term. In general that's true. However, on a risk-adjusted basis, many active managers do outperform the index. Being open-minded helps you see past general rules and take advantage of the details.

Being flexible is key because life doesn't always go the way you think it will. We have a client who is younger; he's not retirement age yet, but he was diagnosed with a disease. We were midway into getting his money into something that was going to lock it down for the long term. This disease, however, is going to require some large payments for medical care, and it's no longer appropriate for us to have that money locked up. So even though we had already done all the work and everything was in place, we scrapped everything, revised the plan, and moved his money somewhere completely different because the circumstances had changed. This kind of flexibility has helped in many other client circumstances because life throws you curveballs, and you need to be able to adapt and react to them.

Take Calculated Risks

It will benefit you in some circumstances to step out of your comfort zone. Many of our clients who are first-time investors have to do this. Some clients are used to putting their money in the bank and they are afraid to move it. Some have it in the bank for years and years, and they finally realize that with inflation, they're actually losing value. So we have the conversation about comfort zones because it scares them to be in the market. They're not comfortable with the potential to lose their funds, but we can build in safety mechanisms. Much of helping people to step outside of that comfort zone comes down to creating the right plan, giving them the confidence to invest, and giving them the right tools.

Build in Fail-Safes

You need safety mechanisms built into your investing behaviors. There were people who lost a lot of money in 2020 because they didn't have the right checks and balances in their investing activities. When we went through the downturn in March 2020, when COVID-19 was really coming into play, we had a very fast crash with an immediate recovery. When the market crashed, some people pulled their funds out because they were scared. They thought the market was going to keep going down, and they didn't want to lose everything. Then they waited until the market got to new highs before they wanted to get back in. This destroys people's investments, but sadly it is very common.

In practice, that's how many investors operate when they don't have the financial knowledge or patience to weather the storm. This is what we're here for: to support people through those down times, to provide the tools they need to weather the storm and manage their behaviors. You see, our value is substantially more than just providing you with an investment portfolio. In fact, when you look at the value of a good financial advisor, on average they're worth somewhere between 3 and 5 percent. Over 1 percent of that comes down to behavior management. One of Warren Buffet's mottos was that you want to be greedy when others are fearful and be fearful when others are greedy. That means keeping your behavior under control and not panicking when everyone else is. We can help you with that by saying, "Hey, I know you want to do this right now, but don't do it." In some ways, we're the equivalent of a marriage counselor for people's financial life.

Take Wise Advice

Another big part of the value of a financial advisor is their training and knowledge. People question whether they should use a financial advisor, partially because all the financial gurus on social media are telling them, "Just buy the index funds; don't pay a financial advisor." This is bad advice because, again, we have tools and knowledge that most people don't have. Now, if you're doing things perfectly, you can do pretty well by following that type of advice, but most people don't. You also need to know that the index is not as well diversified as you believe it is. Seven stocks make up about 30 percent of that index. Personally, I don't like the idea of investing simply based on how big a company is, rather than asking, "Is it a good company? What are the future prospects? Where do they sit today?"

It's good to learn about investing on your own, but know that there are things you don't know, especially the details. Financial advisors have tools in our tool kit that you might not know exist. We can get you into investments that you had no idea were even out there but are a great fit for you.

We also have the time to look deeply into things that you might not have the time to understand completely. For instance, right now annuities are a great example of something that people tend not to understand but that can greatly benefit many investors. Some annuities are absolutely guaranteed[23] no matter what happens in the market, and there's real value in that. Other annuities you can build over time. There are products that limit the downside so that when the market eventually falls, you're protected, but you can grow in a very healthy way when the market is doing well. Once again, the details matter, and it takes expertise to know the details.

Keep Up with Taxes

As your wealth grows, tax management becomes extremely important. Besides behavior management and actual asset allocation, taxes are a major way that financial advisors can add value. This is especially true if they have a background in taxes, as I do. Taxes are important because, at the end of the day, it's what you keep that matters. If you earn 10 percent and you pay 40 percent of that in taxes, you're netting 6 percent. If you earn 9 percent and pay only 2 percent of that in taxes, you net 7 percent. Most people would rather net 7 percent than 6 percent on their money.

---

23 Guarantees are based on the claims paying ability of the issuing company.

Diversify [24]

Lastly, and this is almost a subcategory of its own, most investors need to be very diversified in their portfolios and strategy. There are so many different tools out there that do so many different things for you that you should be taking advantage of. It's my job to make sure my clients benefit from the best tools out there. Here's a sample of the tools we tend to recommend.

Mutual funds tend to be at the top of the list. Over the long term, they tend to be one of the best investments because they don't go through quite as many ebbs and dips as annuities do. However, we don't just do standard mutual funds. Many of the mutual funds we use are actively managed by professional companies. These professionals then are able to ensure that they choose companies in which they have deep convictions, rather than selecting companies simply for their size. There are other investment options similar to mutual funds can offer more tax efficiency or a lower cost. These include separately managed accounts and ETFs.

Separately managed accounts used to have heavy minimums, but they're more widely available now. When they were first created, the minimum was $10 million. Fortunately, these accounts are now affordable for

---

24 There is no guarantee that a diversified portfolio will enhance overall returns or outperform a non-diversified portfolio. Diversification does not protect against market risk.

the average investor. Personal funds can be managed so that taxes are only paid on the realized gains within that portfolio. You can still enjoy a high level of institutional management with research and background details to pick the right stocks for a growth portfolio.

In addition to the tax benefits, we're also able to customize your portfolio for you. So let's say your father passed away from lung cancer, and he was a heavy smoker. You hate tobacco companies. Knowing this, we'll make sure you don't invest in tobacco companies. You don't like alcohol? We can exclude brewers and distillers. You don't like gun companies? We can customize your portfolio in a variety of ways. If you like green energy companies or things of that nature, we can find some good ones. In other words, we can customize your account not only from a tax standpoint but also according to your morals and beliefs, and that's something you can't normally get in a mutual fund.

Tax overlays let us set tax budgets for long-term capital gains so we can limit or even eliminate short-term capital gains and maximize tax loss harvesting, making it a very tax-efficient vehicle. What a lot of people don't realize about mutual funds is that they pay out capital gains distributions, and they do so whether you personally are at a gain or a loss. So you could be down for the year or new to the fund but still have to pay taxes. That doesn't happen in separately managed accounts. In that circumstance, your taxes are based on your individual gain.

A flat trail fee structure allows me to work for you and not myself. When it comes to your tools, there's been a big push—especially over the last ten years—to use "fee-only" advisors. However, fee-only advisors eliminate a huge chunk of the investments that are available. Sometimes a fee-only advisor is great. But there are other times when commission-based products may be more appropriate or lower cost over the long term. I have the ability to adapt to changing environments or circumstances to put you in the investment tools that are best for you at the time you're investing.

Remember that you don't want to artificially limit the diverse set of tools at your disposal. I have no skin in the game when it comes to "brands" or types of tools. Whether you invest with American Funds or Vanguard, I'm getting paid exactly the same. My reason for moving your money to one place versus the other is only that I think it's best for you. With flat trail payment, using the annuities that I'm using today, my payment is generally similar whether I put you in a fee-based account or an annuity. I strive at every step of the way to eliminate or reduce at least the potential for bias related to my compensation

Invest in a More Confident Future

The last key piece of advice in our list of greatest hits is to make investing decisions that will help you and your family pursue your financial goals. One major reason people invest is for their children's education, but there's an even more basic question for investors who have families.

Do you have life insurance? That's one of the first questions I'll ask when we sit down together. We want to make sure that if something happens to you, your spouse and your children can live comfortably. This means we need to be able to replace your income. We look at life insurance first. Typically, we go for term life insurance because it's low cost and effective. Yes, that means you won't have a lifetime guarantee, but life insurance should be looked at in most situations as just that: life insurance. It's there just in case. The goal is that by the time you get to the end of the term on your term life insurance, you're essentially self-insured.

Because of this, what I typically do is set up two life insurance policies using the 4 Percent Rule: Plan to withdraw no more than 4 percent of the policy amount per year. For example, a $1 million policy would provide about $40,000 a year, and maybe we want to replace $60,000 worth of income when the kids are kids, but once they're out of the house, your spouse probably doesn't need that much. In that case, we may issue a twenty-year policy for

$500,000 and a thirty-year policy for $1 million. Then, at the end of twenty years, when your kids are out of the house and hopefully becoming self-sufficient, that first policy drops off and the other policy is to get your spouse into their retirement years. That tends to be the first layer of protection for investors with families. The second layer is retirement savings.

Are you prioritizing retirement savings over education savings? If you're not, I would put your money there first, before opening a 529 education account. You can get financial aid or low-interest subsidized loans for college but typically not for retirement. A 529 account is also directly counted as an asset against you when you're trying to qualify for financial aid. As a result, putting money into a 529 could hurt your ability to get financial aid. Alternatively, if you're already unlikely to qualify and you're already taking care of yourself, that's when I would consider the 529. So then, we build layers: We have term life in case anything happens, we have retirement, and then we have this thing that's basically a stand-in for an educational savings account, it's just a little bit smarter.

Retirement savings and life insurance are basic, but there's another important set of insurance tools: Most people don't plan for or think about (and don't want to think about) long-term care early enough.

Do you have a plan for long-term care?
When most people think about long-term care, they think about an old-age nursing facility, and for a large portion of people who use it, that is accurate. What many people don't realize is it's possible to need long-term care before old age. If you get into an accident and can no longer perform activities of daily living, you may need long-term care. This can come in many forms, including additional help in your own home.

Long-term care isn't cheap. Here in California, it's common for it to cost over $10,000 per month! That's why it's important to consider when planning for long-term prosperity. Long-term care insurance is typically much less expensive if you purchase it when you're young and healthy. As you get closer to retirement age, new coverage often becomes unaffordable. The cost of long-term care isn't likely to go down in the future. Historically, it has been increasing significantly faster than overall inflation. Long-term care coverage can be an important part of your overall financial well-being.

Remember that this is insurance. Sometimes people worry about paying for insurance and not using it. I think this is the wrong way to think about long-term care insurance. You don't buy your car insurance or homeowner's insurance hoping for a car accident or house fire; you are, however, very glad to have it if one of these terrible things happen.

Speaking of homeowner's insurance, most people need to review their coverage to ensure it's enough.

Do you have enough home and auto insurance coverage? In California, the current minimum coverage for auto insurance is $15,000 for injury or death to an individual and $30,000 maximum per accident. This is almost certainly too little insurance. Many vehicles on the road are also far more expensive than the $15,000 limit.

I typically like my own insurance limits to be high enough to cover any potential liability and ensure that the insurance company is vested in defending me if something happens. Insurance companies are in business to make money. If you're in an accident, you want your insurance company on your side. You also want to be sure your coverage is adequate to cover any financial loss you may experience. While I don't personally sell auto or home insurance coverage, I always discuss coverage with clients to ensure they have what they need.

My father's office used to be in Paradise, California. It was lost along with so many offices, homes, and businesses in the Camp Fire in 2018. It was a terrible disaster. Luckily, most of our clients had adequate insurance coverage, which allowed them to either rebuild or purchase new homes. However, I also saw the opposite. I spoke with many victims of the fire who were underinsured, and the loss of their home was financially devastating. Many times, the difference in cost between underinsurance and adequate coverage is minimal, but it can make a large difference in long-term financial success should the worst happen. When you're surveying the financial tools in your toolbox, make sure you don't overlook the value of these different kinds of insurance coverage.

Once you've taken the right steps to protect yourself and your family from disaster, it's time to look at ways to grow your earnings.

Are you invested in the stock market? Direct investment in the stock market is a strong option because it's the best way to achieve growth and offset inflation. The S&P 500 is easy to track. It has averaged about 10 percent per year since its inception, which matches the performance of the stock market as a whole since its inception. Cash, on the other hand, has averaged 3 percent over the long term, and inflation has been the same. Real estate has averaged about 6 percent. So, historically speaking, if I'm looking for the best way to grow my funds, the market has been the best, and I like the odds to be in my favor. It's very hard to lose money when you invest over a ten- or twenty-year period. I call this kind of investment a smart risk.

Beyond that, I like having high-quality, very intelligent investors helping me to pick the best opportunities out there. Because of this, I tend to use a lot of active management,[25] and while most active managers haven't beaten the overall indexes, you have to examine their performance on a risk-adjusted basis. If your portfolio has significantly less risk because you're investing in companies that are more stable, but you're getting a similar return, that's a better scenario.

Do you own cryptocurrency?[26] It's a popular "tool" right now. Personally, I don't typically view currency as an investment and I don't currently own any. I think Bitcoin has great opportunity in the blockchain technology that's behind it. However, for good reason,

---

25 Active portfolio management, including market timing, can subject longer term investors to potentially higher fees and can have a negative effect on the long-term performance due to the transaction costs of the short-term trading. In addition, there may be potential tax consequences from these strategies. Active portfolio management and market timing may be unsuitable for some investors depending on their specific investment objectives and financial position. Active portfolio management does not guarantee a profit or protect against a loss in a declining market.

26 Cryptocurrency is a digital representation of value that functions as a medium of exchange, a unit of account, or a store of value, but it does not have legal tender status. Cryptocurrencies are sometimes exchanged for US dollars or other currencies around the world, but they are not generally backed or supported by any government or central bank. Their value is completely derived by market forces of supply and demand, and they are more volatile than traditional currencies. Cryptocurrencies are not covered by either FDIC or SIPC insurance. Legislative and regulatory changes or actions at the state, federal, or international level may adversely affect the use, transfer, exchange, and value of cryptocurrency.

Purchasing cryptocurrencies comes with a number of risks, including volatile market price swings or flash crashes, market manipulation, and cybersecurity risks. In addition, cryptocurrency markets and exchanges are not regulated with the same controls or customer protections available in equity, option, futures, or foreign exchange investing.

regulators do not allow us to recommend it to our clients. That tells you where they stand. The government could just say tomorrow, "This is illegal." Additionally, with the volatility faced by cryptocurrency, I don't see it as a store of value either.

Another concern about Bitcoin is that there's no value behind it. It's not widely accepted. I can't go down to my local convenience store and pay for my soda with Bitcoin. There are set amounts being released through the blockchain, but an estimated 30 percent of all Bitcoin ever created is gone. This is because people put it in various wallets or other digital storage. If you lose that external wallet, the device you're storing your Bitcoin on, or even just the passcode, there's no way to get it back.

At the end of the day, cryptocurrency is volatile. It's not really an investment. How do I put money into something in order to use it for currency when today it could be worth one hundred dollars, tomorrow it could be worth fifty, and the day after it could be worth two hundred? I'll never know what I can buy with it because it's so unstable. If you're interested in investing in cryptocurrency, my advice is to do it carefully. Limit yourself; don't use more than 5 percent of your portfolio on it because it comes with high risk.

Making the Most of Your Circumstances

Ultimately, growing your wealth and securing your family's future depends on making the most of all your resources. We take a look at your entire financial situation, including your debts, income, and assets. We also look at the tools you have available, which could include 401(k)s, 403(b)s, IRAs, Roth IRAs, and non-qualified investments. We strategize how best to allocate those assets for you. People have different goals and retirement plans. Many want to live different lifestyles. Because of this, we come up with a strategy that's custom-fit to each client to meet their goals and maximize their tax efficiency both now and in the future. That's what we do: We provide the best toolbox of strategies, investments, and advice so you can achieve your goals and make a lasting impact on your world.

All of this might seem like too much information to take in all at once, and for many people, it is. That's one of the reasons I wrote this book: so you can come back to the knowledge and information here time and time again. However, I do think it's important to think about the big picture and remember the major components of a sound financial strategy. This is why I put together a way to make it easier for you to remember what we're doing here.

The FAMILY Planning Process
for Your Finances™

Financial Objectives	We start by understanding your financial objectives and setting clear, measurable goals. This includes defining your time horizon, risk tolerance, and overall financial situation.
Asset Allocations	We design a personalized, diversified investment portfolio tailored to your time horizon, risk tolerance, values, and goals.
Management Philosophy	Our approach combines tax-efficient strategies, active portfolio management, and personalized financial solutions. We continuously monitor and update your plan to ensure it remains aligned with your financial objectives.
Intelligent Risk Protection	We focus on protecting against financial risks that could impact your family's security.
Long-Term Healthcare Planning	We address long-term healthcare needs and explore ways to provide for them.
Your Enduring Prosperity	We help you to create and maintain prosperity for generations to come.

If you look back through the final chapter of this book, I've touched on each of these aspects of the **FAMILY** Planning Process or approach to financial planning. I've explained the importance of sitting down and defining **Financial Objectives** with a qualified advisor. I have outlined principles and strategies for **Asset Allocations.**[27] I've shared the core principles of my **Management Philosophy** for making sound financial decisions. I have emphasized the importance of **Intelligent Risk Protection** as a foundation for your financial security. I've detailed approaches for addressing **Long-Term Healthcare Planning**, which many investors must consider. Together, these form the comprehensive framework of your financial plan and lay the groundwork for building **Your Enduring Prosperity**.

That's what I do for my clients: I help them build enduring prosperity using the incredible variety of tools at my disposal, working alongside them and guiding them with the expertise I've been able to build over the years. I'd love to put this **FAMILY** Planning Process to work for you. Please contact my office, and we'll be happy to help. It's what we love to do. Thank you for allowing me to help you build *A Prosperous Family*.

---

27   Asset allocation does not ensure a profit or protect against a loss.

AFTERWORD

When I set out to write this book, my goal was clear: I didn't want to create another "typical finance book." Instead, I aimed to share real-life stories that taught me valuable lessons, ones you could apply to your own life. My hope was to provide insight into investing and finance without making it a chore to read. After all, wisdom holds value only when we apply it to our lives and take action.

If you're ready to take the next step in building a strong financial foundation and creating a lasting legacy, I hope this book serves as your guide. For those seeking personalized support, I'm just a phone call or email away. It's truly an honor to help you pursue *A Prosperous Family*.

—RJ

ABOUT THE AUTHOR

As the CEO and President of Prosperity Investment Management, Inc., RJ Anderson's primary responsibilities include providing comprehensive financial advice and investment guidance. He specializes in retirement planning and wealth management, with a particular focus on tax-efficient portfolios.

Before joining Prosperity Investment Management, Inc., RJ worked as a Certified Public Accountant® (CPA®) with Tittle and Company and served as the Assistant Superintendent of Business and Operations of Durham Unified School District. These roles provided him with a deep understanding of financial operations and management, preparing him well for his current role. RJ obtained his CPA certification in 2016, further solidifying his expertise in financial management. He graduated with a bachelor's degree from California State University at Chico in 2014, after attending Butte College.

RJ's passion for helping clients reach their financial goals is what drives him. He finds immense satisfaction in seeing others succeed and build their own prosperity. His father, a pillar in the industry for over forty years, built his business on trust and integrity, values RJ has carried forward in his own practice. He says, "The trust that our clients place in us is something I cherish and uphold in all my interactions. What I enjoy most about my job is helping clients invest funds and grow their portfolios. I love providing the security of knowing they're well prepared for retirement. I take pride in customizing plans and portfolios for each individual client, ensuring their unique needs are met."

RJ believes the greatest value he can provide for his clients is helping them find financial peace. He offers investment advice and guidance tailored to their specific scenarios, with a focus on tax efficiency. He says, "After all, it's not just what they make but what they keep that truly matters."

Away from work, RJ lives in his hometown of Chico, California, with his wonderful wife, Michelle, and their children, Lincoln and Charlie. He's a passionate supporter of his children's youth sports teams, firmly believing in the importance of outdoor activities for children. In his free time, RJ enjoys outdoor activities like camping, hiking, biking, skiing, and baseball. He and his family love traveling, having explored various parts of the country and taken trips abroad, creating precious memories while enjoying the great outdoors.

www.ingramcontent.com/pod-product-compliance
Lightning Source LLC
Chambersburg PA
CBHW021458180326
41458CB00051B/6872/J